LINCOLNSHIRE COUNTY
EDUCATION AND CU
This book should b
the last date

02 JAN

16. MAR 04

22 NOV

WITHDRAWN FOR SALE

PT X

WOOLLEY

You can't be serious

822

AD 03750543

Copyright (c) Joan Woolley 1998
The Author asserts the moral right to be identified as the author of this work.

The characters and places in this play are fictional and any similarity between these and those in real life is purely coincidental

Performances or readings of this play may not legally take place before an audience without a licence obtainable on application to:

THE PLAYWRIGHTS PUBLISHING CO.
70 Nottingham Road
Burton Joyce
Notts NG14 5AL
☏ 0115 931 3356

To avoid possible disappointment application should be made, preferably in writing, as early as possible stating:-

(i)   Name and address of applicant

(ii)   Name and address of society

(iii)   Name and address of theatre or hall where the performance would be held

(iv)   Times and dates of performances

A fee will be charged for this licence which must be paid prior to the first performance otherwise the licence is autuomatically cancelled and the performance becomes illegal.

Design and Layout by Wendy Williams of

Eclipse designs

Printing By RPB Print of Burton Joyce Phone/Fax 0115 931 3766

"You Can't Be Serious"

A Tennis Comedy in Two Acts

by
Joan Woolley

The Playwrights Publishing Co

Joan Woolley

A fully-qualified Lawn Tennis Association Professional, having played to national standard and been Sussex and Gloucestershire Singles Champion, co-founded Field Place Junior Tennis Club, Worthing in 1991.

Daughter of a survivor of the Dresden firestorm, visited the city after the demise of the Berlin Wall and later in 1995 as a guest at its 50th year commemorations.

Publications include:

> *DIY Tennis* (Non-fiction)
> *Survival* (Novel - Aftermath of a firestorm)
> *Wanting to Hold the Peace* (Poem - Dresden's 50th anniversary night)
> *Time Slipping Like Sand Through Fingers* (Poem - Remembrance Day)
> *Painter's Pilgrims* (Poem - John Constable)
> *Naked in Public* (Poem - Writing)
> *Peakland Home* (Poem)
> *Swanbourne Lake, Arundel* (Poem)

Currently a professional tennis coach and writer in West Sussex, preparing for the production of her millennium play, a tennis tragicomedy, *Wimbledon or Bust*

"You Can't Be Serious"

First performed by The Barn Theatre Company at the Barn Theatre, Worthing on November 3rd 1997 with the following cast of characters:

Angela Wayward-Jones	*Sonia Spence*
Dudley Strand	*Martin Sworn*
Noreen Bumfrey	*Sonia Johnson*
Lionel Bumfrey	*Gary Krost*
Prudence Noes	*Ceinwen Lloyd*
Violet Lissom-Green	*Mo Russell*
Ronald Murgatroyd	*John Maplesden*
Mr Cattermole	*John Maplesden*
Marlon Tatler	*Jamie Griffiths*
Esme Tipple	*Kay Worthington*
Timothy	*Myles Locke*

Produced by Tony Harris
Directed by Dirk Bollwerk and Peter Massey
Set design by Kenneth Harris   Costumes by Michael Chipper

"You Can't Be Serious"

Character List

Angela Wayward-Jones . . . Hon. Treasurer, Div V Ladies' Captain

Prudence Noes . . . . Honorary Secretary

Lionel Bumfrey . . . Chairman, Men's Captain, Men's Match Secretary

Noreen Bumfrey . . . . Head Coach, Junior Representative

Dudley Strand . . . . Entertainments

Marlon Tatler . . . . Groundsman

Violet Lissom-Green . . . . Vice President

Total Number Characters : 7

Note: Cattermole - Referee, Great Wollop Veterans' Tournament (Played in silhouette with theatre production company supplying voice)

The action of the play takes place in the pavilion of the Little Buttox Lawn Tennis Club and the tennis courts at the Great Wollop Tennis Club

Act One . . . Spring

Act Two . . . Early Summer

Time . . . The Present

YOU CAN'T BE SERIOUS

Little Buttox Lawn Tennis Club

AGENDA FOR MEETING OF THE EXECUTIVE COMMITTEE TO BE HELD IN THE CLUB HOUSE ON

FRIDAY, 1st APRIL AT 7.30 p.m.

1. Minutes of meeting held on 1st April last year
2. Matters arising.
3. Chewing gum.
4. Adjustment of dress code - boxer shorts.
5. Drains. Proposal that a motion be passed.
6. Restricted ladies - Noise interference by groundsman
7. Catering:
   (a) Buns.
   (b) EU legislation and match teas.
   (c) Sandwich fillings for opponents.
   (d) Lost goblets.
8. Tournaments:
   (a) Dudley's Query ... re colour of balls for Floodlit Spag-Bol Tournament.
   (b) Lionel's draws - handicap tournament.
9. Coaching:
   (a) Noreen being certified.
10. Men's and ladies' locker rooms.
    (a) Men's shower curtain.
    (b) Deactivation of keyhole - ladies' locker room
11. Entertainments:
    (a) Little Buttox Vegetarian Ball.
    (b) Fondle Party.
    (c) Pat and Punch Party.
12. A.O.B.

Prudence Noes

Hon. Secretary

NOTE TO COMMITTEE MEMBERS

Lionel has a big agenda. Whilst every effort will be made, it may not be possible to fit it all in. Please stick to relevant matters only. No time wasting please.

YOU CAN'T BE SERIOUS
A Tennis Comedy in Two Acts

ACT 1
Scene 1

(Note to Marketing Department of Theatre Company: You may wish to add a note on the tickets and pre-show publicity material to the following effect - "If you are a member of the tennis fraternity, or simply would have pleasure in doing so, it would be much enjoyed if you attended the show dressed in sporting attire, as the cast wish to make you feel part of the hotbed world of Little Buttox Lawn Tennis Club." If the facility was available locally, may be the Little Buttox Morris Dancing Group performing at entrance to theatre)

SCENE. - The curtains are open. L is a trestle table with an odd assortment of chairs for use by Little Buttox executive committee. L is door of main club entrance. The area just outside the door can be seen. A red light illuminates the pathway. R is a bar area. L of this at back of stage is a door which leads to the kitchen, changing rooms and back entrance to club house. R of bar area is door to broom cupboard. Below stage on green baize is a short tennis court with net over which members of production company are playing tennis with soft balls. They are dressed as tennis players and invite members of audience to join them. Tennis music is playing. Copies of the 'The Little Buttox Gazette' are for sale at the theatre bar. Inside is information about the theatre company who is producing the show and any items of local news they wish their visitors to know. Tennis club merchandise could be for sale e.g. Little Buttox Tennis Club t-shirts, sweatshirts and tennis balls with Little Buttox LTC rubber stamped on.

It is April. Wooden pavilion. Large trestle table is piled with papers. Photos of past teams on wall. Yellowing trophies. Little Buttox is pronounced Little Boottox by Angela and Violet; Little Buttox by other members.

The interchanges between club members should be fast as though they are volleying furiously at each other at the net. These people know each other and some of their foibles extremely well and so cut in with what they wish to say before the other person has finished speaking. It is a great pleasure when they succeed in outrallying each other and achieve the final winning verbal lob or dropshot.

(See Ground Plan)

YOU CAN'T BE SERIOUS

DUDLEY *(Squeaking of bicycle. A figure in dark cloak wheels bicycle up auditorium aisle to stage. Makes a big thing of putting lock and chain on. Leaves bicycle below L and mounts the steps to the stage and club entrance L. Tchaikovsky's 'Dance of the Sugar-Plum Fairy' plays. Enters clubhouse. Stage dimly lit. Takes cloak and some other smock-like garment off and hangs them on the row of pegs inside club entrance door. Switches light on. Looks down at ankles. Takes off cycle clips and hangs them on a special peg. Dressed in cardigan and twill trousers. Rubs hands together as he strides across the clubhouse floor to switch a heater on. After doing so, looks at one of the photos on the wall Effete voice)* Ah the Bognor Tennis Tournament. I remember it well. Still every tennis player should have their day. *(Surreptitious look around. Rummages in a cupboard and draws out half-finished knitting. Sits down at end of committee table furthest from door and with a huge sigh of contentment begins to knit)*

PRUDENCE *(Roar of motorbike. 'The Typewriter' by Leroy Anderson plays. A figure in long smock scurries down auditorium aisle. Under one arm is a motorcycle helmet and the hand of that arm holds a bag designed for papers; the other hand flaps around as she scuttles. Enters club entrance. Little girl voice. Giggles a lot)* Hello Dudley. How did you get on in your knitting competition?

DUDLEY Came second to Noreen. I'm not speaking to her.

PRUDENCE It's not going to be one of those meetings. Our treasurer not here yet?

DUDLEY As you can hear, Angela is not here yet. Mother well?

PRUDENCE Gone to bingo but getting back early to finish a tea cosy. Wants me home quickly 'cos she doesn't like being alone with her Horlicks.

DUDLEY You're a good girl. Goodness knows where you get it from, I mean, sorry, you know what I mean...the influence of us lot.

PRUDENCE *(Prissy walk. Puts motorcycle helmet in broom cupboard R. Bustles around emptying ashtrays, picking up litter from floor. Picks up loo brush from floor and puts on trophy shelf)* Oh.

DUDLEY My dear Prudence, as you so eloquently say, 'Oh.'

(Whilst Prudence sits at end of table nearest club entrance, gets out her papers, sticks her tongue out as she writes, makes a big fuss about starting a new page in her shorthand notebook and sharpening pencils and Dudley

knits, the sound of a vehicle on its last legs is heard. It shudders to a halt. The song 'One man went to mow, went to mow a meadow' is heard. Young man in workman's attire i.e. jeans, plaid shirt, waistcoat, cap back to front walks down auditorium aisle. Enters clubhouse)

DUDLEY   Hello Marlon.

PRUDENCE   Hello Marlon *(She is deep in her paperwork so does not see look of adoration from Marlon as he sidles up to her and says in rural accent)*

MARLON   Hello Prudence. Hello Dudley.

DUDLEY   How's mother?

MARLON   I can't stay long because I've got to put a shelf up for her. *(Starts measuring door frame by putting a hand at one end of it and the other hand at the other end, then walking towards another door, keeping his hands that distance apart)*

DUDLEY   What on earth are you doing, Marlon?

MARLON   I'm measuring. *(How can you be so stupid tone)*

DUDLEY   It doesn't look very scientific to me.

MARLON   I haves me ways. *(Sits down next to Prudence. Watches as she concentrates on her work.*

(Roar of motorbike. Revving. Expletive. 'Arrival of Queen of Sheba' music plays. Magnificent specimen of a woman in middle years, dressed in black leather skirt and jacket suit with low cut red top and inappropriately high heels and carrying a red motorcycle crash helmet teeters seductively down auditorium aisle to enter L Flings clubhouse door open and makes an entrance)

ANGELA   Can't stay long. I've got a date.

DUDLEY   Have you? *(Looks unhappy about it)*

PRUDENCE   Good.

ANGELA   Pardon?

MARLON   She said 'good.'

YOU CAN'T BE SERIOUS

ANGELA *(Momentary look of hurt on Angela's face. Removes leather jacket. Seats herself centre back of trestle table. Gets out make-up bag from handbag. Begins a serious manicure and general preen)* Without me, darlings you couldn't run a whelk stall.

(Telephone rings. Rimsky-Korsakov's 'Flight of the Bumble Bee' music in background)

PRUDENCE *(Gets up to answer telephone which is mounted on the wall R of club entrance. She picks telephone off the wall, puts up the aerial. Below stage R lit)* Little Buttox Lawn Tennis Club. Secretary speaking. *(Little girl voice)*

ANGELA *(Rolls eyes to heavens. Filing nails)* Gawd.

(R and almost part of the audience is an area indicating Lionel's sitting room. He is on the telephone with his back to the audience. On back of tracksuit top is written 'Little Buttox LTC Men's Captain' He then sits down in chair to talk to Prudence)

LIONEL speaking.   Put a sock in it, Prudence. This is your chairman

PRUDENCE   Oh hello Lionel. *(Covers 'phone. To Committee)* It's Lionel.

COMMITTEE   *(General groan)*

LIONEL   Tell the committee I'll be there in two bangs of a tennis ball, only the wife's lost the addendum to Section 13 of Clause 26 about the adjustment to dress code, oh and can you remove my men's draws to the bottom of the agenda and stick chewing gum on? By the way, is Angela there? *(Ends much of his conversation with a lecherous snort of a laugh)*

PRUDENCE   *(Now seated left of Angela. Looks disgustedly at Angela's impressive and exposed cleavage)* You can hardly miss her.

LIONEL   Is she wearing her low cut...*(pause)*...you know...?

ANGELA *(Angela who is filing her nails and earwigging into the handset hears this)* Cheeky man.

PRUDENCE   If you mean inappropriately dressed, yes. *(To committee)* Can't find his addendum or something. *(General groan from committee)*

ANGELA *(Rich plummy voice)* Let's hope his *little* addendum stays lost.

LIONEL What's that Noreen? *(Shouting to someone at the back of the auditorium who shouts back)* Oh it's O.K. we've found it. Can you tell the committee, Noreen's put it in a safe place. It was next to the salmon in the freezer.

(Lionel replaces receiver. Lights below stage R off)

PRUDENCE Yes Lionel. *(To committee)* He says his addendum's in the freezer.

ANGELA Good heavens, from rigid agenda to frigid addenda, whatever next. For God's sake shut him up or we'll be sitting in this wooden shack all night and this treasurer for one, has a hot date with a good-looking tennis coach called Timothy pending on the agenda. Given the choice of treading through treacle and one of these committee meetings, well need I say more...

PRUDENCE Good.

DUDLEY *(Pauses unhappily with his knitting)*

ANGELA I don't know what you're so pleased about?

PRUDENCE *(Ignores)* Lionel says can you drop his draws to the bottom of the agenda and stick chewing gum on and not to discuss anything important until he and Noreen arrive.

ANGELA Are you sure he said that?

PRUDENCE Well something like that. *(Returns to seat after replacing the telephone)*

ANGELA I like to harvest the expertise of experts. In the temporary absence of our chairman and as I am responsible for dispensing largess, may I ask you, Marlon, in your capacity as groundsman, why the drains go up to the river and not down?

MARLON *(Rural accent. Slow speaking. Offended tone)* How should I know? My mother's not well, my mower's not working, I'm under the doctor as it is and if I'm not paid more I'm not mowing more than once a week *and* last Friday I was stung in the hollyhocks.

ANGELA   *(Leaning forward seductively)* I wish you'd damn well stop mowing during restricted ladies morning.

MARLON   *(Fed up)* What *are* restricted ladies ?

ANGELA   *(Impatient)* They're lady members who get in on the cheap because they play in off peak times and we're about to lose those because they're complaining about your noises. I want to pass a motion *(pause)* that mowing does not take place during restricted ladies' morning?

MARLON   It's the only time I can do it. I don't see why I should be restricted. I'm under the doctor as it is.

ANGELA   We're all under the doctor, darling.

DUDLEY   And you more than most.

ANGELA   Thank you for that, Dudley, my darling. Envy from the entertainments section is always appreciated. *(Turns to Prudence who is writing in her pad)* No, Prudence, don't record that in the minutes. I know you take everything down at these meetings. Good heavens, what on earth have you got on? Is it a milking smock?

MARLON   *(Fed up)* And what's wrong with a milking smock? *(To Prudence)* Very becoming I think. *(To Committee)* That reminds me I've just applied for a job as part-time relief milker to two hundred cows 'cos *you* lot don't pay me enough.

PRUDENCE   *(Reads from Little Buttox Gazette)* Two hundred cows doesn't sound very part-time. *(Reading)* Is it this one next to Noreen's advert in the *Little Buttox Gazette* for an assistant coach? Male stroke female?

DUDLEY   *(Effete voice)* Would suit me with my hours.

PRUDENCE   *(Reading)* Disgusting. I didn't think it was that sort of paper.

ANGELA   *(Examining a finger-nail)* And what pray is Disgusted of Little Boottox disgusted about this time?

PRUDENCE   *(Reading)* Gay lady, own transport, hobbies soft furnishings and eating out at garden centres seeks similarly inclined.

ANGELA   *(To Prudence)* What's disgusting about eating out at garden centres?

PRUDENCE   You know what I mean.

ANGELA   Of course I know what you mean. I should give her a ring. You never know it may be the answer to all your problems. Can I have a look at your *Gazette?*

PRUDENCE   If you lived with my mother you'd have problems.

ANGELA   You never know what problems other people have until you get to know them.

PRUDENCE   No you can't have a look at my *Gazette*. Mother hasn't finished reading it and she doesn't want your doodles all over it again.

ANGELA   Oh suit yourself. *(Gets up. Sways seductively over to shelf with magazines and newspapers on it. Dudley glances up from knitting, then with unhappy look goes back to it)* Anyway back to drains. The court backing onto Boottox End i.e. Violet's house, floods when it's spring tide at Boottox Lock and it's always spring tide when I'm playing my handicap singles. *(Rifles through piles of papers and magazines)* I hope our Vice President, Violet's not going to burst in here clutching her agenda.

DUDLEY   She's no reason to.

ANGELA   She's been odd lately.

PRUDENCE   Mrs Lissom-Green's always odd.

ANGELA   She's been odder.

PRUDENCE   She's got the best interests of the club at heart.

ANGELA   When you're older you'll learn that a human being is programmed to survive and that means having one's *own* best interests at heart.

PRUDENCE   Sounds a bit hard.

ANGELA   She's up to something. Funny how every club she's been a member of closes down and the land is sold and Violet always seems in a position to cop some of the loot.

PRUDENCE   You were a member of those clubs.

ANGELA   True, dear, but then I had the best interests of the club at heart. Don't you just adore reading the adverts in the *Gazette*. *(Wanders around clubhouse reading from Gazette, finally going behind the bar and leaning her bust on the bar counter)* Middle Boottox Sterile Services. Assistant wanted. Equipment not essential. Can be sterilised on site. *(Shaking head)* Sounds drastic. Can I have a rematch? I slipped at five-all on the Boottox End court. If I hadn't slipped who knows. *(Reading)* Strippers and fitters wanted for Little Boottox Body Repair Shop. We ought to book this executive committee in. 'Cept her of course. Not enough mileage on *her* clock. *(Nodding towards Prudence who does not notice)*

PRUDENCE   *(Writing in notepad)* Buttox End.

DUDLEY   I'd like to know who put the drains in.

ANGELA   A former executive committee whose bodies now lie under the sod and probably under Boottox End court judging by all the trouble it gives us. *(Picks up agenda)* Talking of agenda, Prudence, I like the sound of a Fondle Party and a Pat and Punch Party.

PRUDENCE   *(Looks at agenda. Giggles)* Oh dear. I am afraid that was a typographical error. It should be Fondue Party and Pate and Punch Party. Sorree. *(High-pitched giggle which Angela imitates at various points during the meeting)*

ANGELA   Another of your cock-ups you mean. I should leave it as it is, dear. You'll get a bigger and more interesting crowd. *(Reading)* *The Little Boottox Gazette common*ly known as *The Sleaze Gazette* is getting quite modern.

PRUDENCE   It is *common*. Deals with the sort of things you deal with working in *that* clinic.

ANGELA   *(Mimics Prudence's voice and walks over to stand over her)* Oh we're very modern working in *that* clinic. Some people do useful things in the community like saving fallen women instead of baking infernal award-winning chocolate cakes like Noreen. I wonder if we'll be spared this evening. *(Reading)* I see our Vice-President's piece on spanking's in. *(Reading)* *The Little Boottox Gazette*'s reporter, wishing to speak with the village's leading thespian called upon Violet Lissom-Green. Mrs Lissom-Green *(Thrusts bust out)* attired in riding clothes and carrying a riding crop, on being asked her views upon the proposal to make smacking between thespians illegal asserted that, *(Mimics Violet's voice)* '*We're all thespians in Little Boottox and will continue to spank on stage until the Court of Strasbourg decrees otherwise.*' Regarding as to what would happen should a ban be enforced, she reassured the *Gazette* that '*Little*

Boottox members were well in hand to march on Downing Street.' Anyway I digress.

PRUDENCE   What's new?

ANGELA   What's that, darling? Do speak up. Can we agree I find out who put the drains in and get three estimates regarding the cost of rectifying the situation?

PRUDENCE   Can I pass a motion *(Pause)* that if anyone is not prepared to make cakes they shouldn't be in the team?

ANGELA   Oh that's ridiculous. Look unless we get these drains sorted, *no one* will be passing a motion. I'll scream if I have to face one more of Noreen's award winning chocolate cakes. I haven't bent like a young sapling for my smashes for ages.

DUDLEY   Some of us haven't *been* a young sapling for ages.

ANGELA   Some of us never *were*.

PRUDENCE   *(Pencil raised hopefully)* Have I missed something?

ANGELA   More than you'll ever know, darling. So have we decided on the drains?

DUDLEY   Who do I ask about a rematch? *I* was on Buttox End court as well. I'd have won if I'd been able to keep myself upright.

PRUDENCE   Talking of water on Buttox End court, being in insurance, I would say the tidal system comes under an act of God, so you'll just have to put up with it.

ANGELA   *(Signs of boredom)* Can he insure against boredom?

PRUDENCE   You can insure against anything. Unfortunately not against having people like you on committees.

ANGELA   Thank you. When people are bitchy I know they're envious. Vice President, Violet didn't get anything when the Great Wollop Marathon was diverted through her garden. She was peacefully hanging out her *(hand signs indicating small)* smalls and by the time they'd gone, she was round the back of the potting shed with a couple of runners.

MARLON   Yea, Mrs Floggitt at the stores told the milkman who told my mum. My mum says you probably gave a helping hand.

ANGELA   (*Examining nails*) Tell her there wasn't time, dear. Violet's beehives went over and the bees got the upper hand. I told her to slap an onion on her bum to get the swelling down. Seems a waste really when you think how much people fork out for the beestung look.

PRUDENCE   That's for on the lips.

(*Enter Lionel to 'Flight of the Bumble Bee' dressed in tracksuit, tennis headband round head and carrying a display board*)

ANGELA   Oh God it's the Errol Flynn of the ball bearing world. Won a holiday to Florida for selling the most ball-bearings on the south coast.

LIONEL   Evenin' all. Well this time tomorrow, I'll be in sunny Florida.

ANGELA   Accompanied by Hurricane Noreen I suppose.

LIONEL   (*Takes off tracksuit top, revealing a garish floral shirt. Whoops of appreciation from committee members. Sits between Marlon and Angela. He puts pencil case down on table and with eyes fixed onto Angela's bust he speaks. Angela is turned towards him*) Now, this week, I have commenced my investigations (*Eyes focussed on Angela's bust*) about removing chewing gum from the bitumen court surface. I have to warn you it's going to take a big part of our budget.

ANGELA   (*Manicuring nails*) Oh come on man spit it out. I've got pressing engagements with bosom pals even if you haven't. How much and I'll let you know if you can have it. By the way, where's Noreen. (*Hand on Lionel's knee*) You and Noreen seen the wisdom of separate committee rooms?

LIONEL   (*Without enthusiasm*) She's on her way. In fact, I got not three estimates, but four! (*Squeal of delight from Angela*) Apparently the Little Buttox Council has had similar problems trying to cleanse its local amenities of chewing gum.

ANGELA   After a sports injuries and massage course, the Little Boottox Council asked if I'd like to become a local amenity.

LIONEL   You went freelance.

ANGELA   (*Varnishing her finger-nails*) Nothing like strumming your own tune.

PRUDENCE   Even on a clapped-out old fiddle like you.

ANGELA   I can't imagine anyone's even *played* a tune on you.

('Love and Marriage' begins to play. Enter Noreen through the auditorium, dropping papers and files and wailing as she goes. Dressed in tracksuit with 'Little Buttox Coach' on jacket back. Amid banging and thumping, Noreen tumbles in L, festooned with carrier bags a briefcase, an old-fashioned handbag and balancing a cake tin. Just outside club entrance the cake tin crashes to ground)

ANGELA   *(To committee)* Lionel's bag lady. *(Shouts to Noreen)* Is that your award winning chocolate cake, Noreen, dear?

NOREEN   Damn and blast it is.

ANGELA   *(Smiling happily to other members)* What a shame. It'll be inedible then?

NOREEN   Oh no, don't worry, it'll be fine.

ANGELA   Oh...uh..good.

(Enter Noreen. Goes towards seat between Dudley and Angela. Drops all her bags and papers. Cry of exasperation. Marlon gets up to help her)

NOREEN   So sorry I'm late. I filed the smoked salmon under D for dress and the addendum in the freezer. I remembered about the salmon when water started coming out of the filing cabinet.

ANGELA   *(Squeal of delight)* Panic attacks; inability to cope. Menopause old dear. Takes some like that.

NOREEN   Menowhat? Oh women's things. Oh...*(Giggling)*...*I'm* still firing on all cylinders.

ANGELA   How inconvenient. Sounds like you ought to be down at one of my birth control workshops.

NOREEN   You're a fine one to talk.

DUDLEY   I propose the whole summer singles championship be replayed. What with tidal flotsam on Buttox End court, American gum disease and court four being a metre shorter at the far end; I think it makes our results null and void.

ANGELA   You've never once got past the first round.

DUDLEY   *(Offended)* I've taken on a professional this time.

ANGELA   *(Looking in mirror)* So that's what all that extra technical work with Noreen's new assistant coach, Timothy, was in aid of? Talk about Greek gods. Isn't he *gorgeous*?

PRUDENCE   *(High-pitched voice)* Shall I take that down?

ANGELA   I can't imagine you taking anything down. I think of you whenever I see those refrigerated vans. Your pussy gets more attention than any human being.

PRUDENCE   Mrs Wayward-Jones, I don't mean to be rude, and I know you move in literary circles, but why don't you say things people wouldn't misunderstand? Anyway, what better company than your own cat? *(Impressively)* Anyway, *I* went out with a policeman once.

ANGELA   *(Dismissively)* I bet you didn't let him take down *your* particulars. You probably bashed him over the head with your handbag and said, *(Mimicking Pru's voice)* 'your feelings are not reciprocated, please keep them to yourself young man.' *(Mimics Prudence's girly giggle then reflectively)* Actually you might be O.K. with a policeman. Beware young men offering to buy you fish and chips on Bognor Pier.

PRUDENCE   What's she talking about Dudley?

DUDLEY   *(Looks embarrassed. Stops his knitting. Looks nostalgic for a moment. Recovers)* Don't ask me. I'm more your hand holding type.

ANGELA   *(Mimicking Dudley)* All I can do is hold you. That should be etched on your gravestone.

DUDLEY   We're not all like you, darling.

ANGELA   You mean I've got hot blood pounding through my veins and not enough people to stir it.

DUDLEY   Well you're certainly unconventionaL

PRUDENCE   What's she talking about? I've completely lost my thread now.

ANGELA   Her flat's like a chastity belt. More locks than a canal. *(Looking at Marlon)* You'll be past it, Marlon, by the time you get anywhere *near* her chest of drawers.

NOREEN   Ignore her, Prudence. She's got a grudge against the human race. I'm not surprised her mother chucked her out.

PRUDENCE   Don't you think it's time you came to terms with it, Mrs Wayward-Jones? We've all got problem areas in our relationships with our mothers.

ANGELA   *(Mellifluous cooing noise)* Oho?

PRUDENCE   Mind your own business.

ANGELA   Since nothing seems to have happened to you between your teens and thirties, one wouldn't expect you to get your head round the nuances of emotional life.

LIONEL   Right boys and girls. Drain estimates.

PRUDENCE   *(Writing)* Drain estimates. I'm sure I've missed something?

ANGELA   You certainly have. They ought to put a frostbite warning on you.

PRUDENCE   *(Stands up)* I've had enough. I'm not staying here to be insulted.

ANGELA   Oho, temper, temper.

PRUDENCE   There are better things I could be doing tonight.

ANGELA   Oh yeah? Knitting a tea cosy are we?

PRUDENCE   You know the difference between you and the Eiffel Tower?

ANGELA   Do tell us darling. If it's anything to do with more tourists having been up, I've heard it. Old as the hills, that one.

PRUDENCE   Shows your age that you *know* it's old as the hills.

ANGELA   *(Rising wrathfully from seat)*

DUDLEY   *(Rising in seat)* Ladies, ladies, please. Why can't we all be nice to each other?

LIONEL   Look, seriously folks, if we can't pass a motion on the drains, I vote we stick to chewing gum.

ANGELA   Now you're talking. *(Sits down. Leans seductively towards Lionel)* Lionel, before you begin your thesis on chewing gum, may I interrupt.

LIONEL   You can interrupt me any time you like.

NOREEN   *(Warningly)* Lionel stop it.

ANGELA   By the way, Marlon, how did you come to be called Marlon?

MARLON   Me dad took me mum to see Marlon Brando in *A Streetcar Named Desire.*

ANGELA   Let me guess. She came out inflamed with desire.

MARLON   Yeah. How did you know?

ANGELA   Oh feminine intuition? *(In experienced tones. Looking down at herself and flicking a fleck of dust off)* You'll understand when you experience an experienced woman.

MARLON   Mother said not to tamper with older women.

NOREEN   From what I hear about a certain treasurer's interests *(Looking pointedly at Angela)*, let's hope my assistant coach's mum has told him not to tamper with older women.

ANGELA   And they don't come more tamperproof than you. I think it's wonderful the way human life meanders along. I mean how many tennis clubs have got someone called Marlon tying up their hollyhocks.

MARLON   Mother says you're lucky to have me.

ANGELA   *(Imitates Marlon's rural accent)* And that you're worth your weight in gold. *(Own voice)* But we simply haven't got the budget to fund all your Capability Brown landscapes. I can run to a few extra pansies *(rural accent)* but not an extra mow.

DUDLEY Have we agreed then? Summer singles championships to be replayed? *(General outcry as every member puts in his/her demands regarding the summer tournament. Lionel stands up and yells at the top of his voice. Prudence shrieks. Angela, impressed at his dominance, hums her approval)*

LIONEL Can we stick to my chewing gum, only Nor and me are due at a beetle drive. It doesn't seem to go if we're not there.

ANGELA Things always go with a bang when Li's in town.

LIONEL *(Gets up. Goes to front of stage with extending ruler. Puts up his display board. Flicks over pages of amusing drawings depicting people stepping into dog muck, chewing gum adhering to people's shoes, restricted ladies to illustrate talk)* I'll illustrate my talk with a little something I prepared beforehand. Chappie I know's invented a machine for clearing up dog wotsits on Little Buttox and Great Wollop parks. He's moving fast into chewing gum. We can borrow it. But ...

ANGELA Go on then. Tell us the worst.

LIONEL They do want a favour in return.

DUDLEY Maybe Angela could help us out. She's very good with council members.

ANGELA Cheeky. I'll sort you out later.

DUDLEY Wasting your time, dearie. *(Triumphantly)* I'm meeting our new coach, Timothy at the new wine bar.

NOREEN *Assistant* coach. I'm the coach.

ANGELA Ambition of youth snapping at your heels, Noreen? Don't bank on it, Dudley. Our Timothy's only ten per cent reliable and I think you'll find it's me he's meeting.

DUDLEY *(Looking unhappy)* Oh.

LIONEL In return for their dog wotsits machine, the Little Buttox Council want to use some of our courts free of charge on Sunday evenings.

ANGELA But *that's* one of our restricted ladies' time.

LIONEL Exactly. This is my master plan. We've a lot of single and restricted ladies. Damn good for bar takings if these non-members came in. *(Flicks onto drawing of someone taking someone's bra)* Oh honestly, Noreen I wanted you to illustrate bar takings not bra takings.

NOREEN I could do my award winning chocolate cake?

ANGELA *(Witheringly)* Oh that'll pull them in. What Sunday evening? It'll take more than award winning chocolate cake and some fresh-blooded non-members to prize those sensible-shod ladies out of their pack-a-macs and fawn locknit knickers.

PRUDENCE *(Offended)* I go to all the Sunday practices.

ANGELA Exactly. You're a bloody miracle.

PRUDENCE Pardon?

ANGELA It's a bloody miracle someone so boring could actually exist.

PRUDENCE That's it. I'm never coming to one of your meetings again. You're all so cruel to each other. I like nice people. *(Prudence rushes out sobbing R to broom cupboard)*

ANGELA Wrong exit, Prudence dear, you're in the broom cupboard.

(Prudence holding handkerchief to her nose, rushes across stage to kitchen rear R)

LIONEL Can't somebody do something? Dudley, you understand women.

(Marlon and Dudley rush through kitchen door after Prudence)

ANGELA I can't think how.

DUDLEY *(Poking head round kitchen door)* Honestly, Ange, you go too far sometimes. She's not in your league.

ANGELA *(Sullenly)* She needs to grow up. What'll she do when Mummy's not there?

DUDLEY   Just lighten up, that's all. She can't go home. Her mum's at bingo, and she doesn't have her own key. Just 'cos you were unlucky with your mother, some people have good relationships with theirs.

LIONEL   *(Proudly)* I did.

NOREEN   She didn't think so.

DUDLEY   *(Dudley enters from kitchen door leading Prudence)* Now, Ange, say you're sorry or else I'll offer to partner you in the club tournament.

ANGELA   *(Sulkily)* You certainly know how to frighten a woman. *(Gets up. Teeters sexily on her white sling back high heels. Wearing black stockings and black leather shirt. Goes to kitchen to get Prudence. As she approaches kitchen door)* Prudence, darling, sorree. *(Returns shepherding a sniffling Prudence in front of her)* Sorry, Prudence. Bad day and all that.

PRUDENCE   *(Hopefully and dabbing nose with tissue)* Friends again, then?

ANGELA   Hardly. *(Clearing throat)* Uh, yes.

PRUDENCE   *(Sits down. Sniffing)* I've put the kettle on. *(General hum of appreciation)*

LIONEL   *(Angela is sandwiched between Noreen and Lionel. When a husband and wife volley of retorts occurs, Angela's heads move back and forth like a tennis match)* What do you mean about my mother? I was the apple of her eye.

NOREEN   Exactly and we've all been paying for it ever since.

LIONEL   My mother said whoever got me would be a lucky woman.

NOREEN   Well your mother always was an optimist.

DUDLEY   Look about the Little Boottox Council having three courts on Sunday evenings. That's a nice compromise, isn't it? All agreed?

NOREEN   *(To Lionel across Angela)* You only see things from your own point of view. She was just someone to do everything for you. You never saw her as a human being; someone with needs. I have needs. Not every person's needs are the same as yours.

ANGELA   *(To Lionel on her left)* Mine are.

NOREEN   Keep your nose out of this you..you.. floozie *(Angela wipes face and moves back out of the line of fire)*

ANGELA   *(Admiringly)* Nice one. *(Adjusting her bra strap)* Least I don't need WD40 to undo the wing nuts on my bra. *(Fingering Lionel's shirt sleeve)* I'll bet you have some lovely rows. *(Dreamily)* And then there's all the making up afterwards.

NOREEN   We've all got our own agenda you know. At our age, some things begin to stick in your craw. And you...*(To Angela)*...get right up my nose, and...*(To Lionel)*...so do you.

LIONEL   *(Patronizingly)* Agenda. Ever since she started going to that women's group, it's agenda this and agenda that. Look if we've sorted the chewing gum, and we're deferring drains to another meeting...

ANGELA   Like the next millennium.

LIONEL   ...How about a coffee break?

(Signs of approval from members. No one moves)

ANGELA   I'll lay fifty quid it's a human being shaped like a woman who makes the first move towards the kettle.

(Noreen gets up, moves behind Angela until she reaches Lionel)

LIONEL   That's why women have smaller feet, so they can get closer to the sink. *(Lecherous snort)*

NOREEN   *(Swipes him over the head with rolled copy of Little Buttox Gazette. To Lionel)* And another thing. I don't see why because I'm shaped like a woman...

ANGELA   The wonder of delusion.

NOREEN   *(Black look at Angela)*...I get to do the washing up, the dirty linen, the cooking and...and...all the unimportant stuff...*(Goes into kitchen)*

ANGELA   While he sits in Rome fiddling with his addenda and preening himself like Narcissus.

LIONEL   *(Calling to kitchen)* I got Emma for you. *(Enter Noreen, arms folded for combat)*

ANGELA   *(Intrigued)* Who's Emma? The au pair? Is she dishy?

NOREEN   *(Emerging from kitchen. Snapping)* Dishy all right. A washing up machine. You know what we agreed when we married? Equality in all things.

ANGELA   No such thing, dearie.

NOREEN   *(Hopefully)* I've got a little treat for you all. I've brought some of my award winning chocolate cake. *(Gets up and exits to kitchen Everyone groans. Pokes her head through kitchen door. Everyone quickly changes the groan to shows of enthusiasm for her chocolate cake)* I'll do the teas and coffees. Unfortunately Lionel likes me old-fashioned. *(Goes into kitchen)*

ANGELA   Good job.

NOREEN   *(Pokes head round kitchen door)* Who's for coffee. Who's for tea.

LIONEL   Hands up for tea. *(Counts)* Three of each, Noreen. Thank you.

NOREEN   *(Pokes head round kitchen door)* Will we be much longer?

LIONEL   If we can get on without the chit-chat, not much longer. *(Taps watch)* Time, Nor, time. Beetle drive.

NOREEN   They can manage without us. They said they had a really wonderful evening last time - shame we missed it.

LIONEL   Disorganised and boring I heard.

ANGELA   Was Prudence there then?

DUDLEY   *(Warningly to Angela)* I think you're due for a *Be Nice to Prudence Week* as she's just been made chairman of the Draws Committee.

NOREEN   *(Poking head round kitchen door)* Sort of committee you ought to be on, Angela. Your knickers contravene EU legislation. *(Enters from kitchen door. Sits down. Tucks paper serviette into neckline.*

Addresses her chocolate cake with enthusiasm whilst others are offering theirs to Marlon who is eating furiously and nodding his head. Angela is trying to fit hers into her handbag)

(Wagner's 'Ride of the Valkyries' plays. Splash. Scream)

ANGELA Hark I hear the arrival of our president of vice.

DUDLEY I knew she'd never get over the ditch from her garden at night. It's only a plank.

MARLON I put a hand rail on it exactly like what you said I should do.

ANGELA And now it's had a test run you can hear the fruits of your labours.

LIONEL I like robust women.

ANGELA I thought your hobby was tennis?

NOREEN Stamp collecting, train-spotting and robust women. *You* should know.

(Enter down auditorium aisle Vice-President Violet in violet-hued jumpsuit, wet, muddy and dishevelled, carrying a file of papers and a handrail)

VIOLET *(Mounts steps L and into clubhouse door. Silently she hands the handrail to Marlon who looks sheepish. Violet glares at committee as they try valiantly not to look amused)* Well I'm glad to see you're not all at home with a headache like last time. Please exhibit your agenda.

(Everyone gets up to rummage in a bag or under the table)

NOREEN *(Exhibits a packet of salmon from her handbag. Triumphant)* I knew I'd put a third packet of salmon somewhere.

LIONEL *(Irritable)* Oh Noreen.

VIOLET *(Hitches herself with difficulty onto a barstool by bar counter)* Now I want you all to pretend I'm not here. It is necessary to sit in on some of your meetings to check you're conforming to all the new EU legislation. I've got reams of it here. Now Dudley.

DUDLEY Yes Violet *(Almost stands to attention)*

VIOLET	If you bring mayonnaise to the club I want you to photograph the date stamp. EU legislation.

DUDLEY	Why?

VIOLET	We are now obliged not to poison visiting teams as part of our match tactics.

NOREEN	Doesn't matter about us then.

VIOLET	Don't be silly Noreen. What with that B.O.F. from Brussels coming, there's an awful lot to do. Actually, Noreen, dear, if you will insist upon supplying us with award winning chocolate cakes I'll need a list of ingredients. EU legislation.

NOREEN	*(Frostily)* Oh.

VIOLET	*(Menacingly)* O.K. ya?

ANGELA	About time too. They ought to check you're not poisoning us all.

NOREEN	Bastards.

LIONEL	Noreen.

ANGELA	*(Touching up her lipstick. Looking into a mirror)* Brussels are closing in you know. It's EU this, EU that, and EU you do this, and EU you do that.

PRUDENCE	I think there's going to be a revolution before the year's out. *(Writing)* Is B.O.F. another of your committee terms?

ANGELA	*(Checking lipstick in mirror)* It means boring old fart. I expect Noreen's women's group are preparing for a revolution.

DUDLEY	I'll be redundant soon. They're making great strides in my profession. Not the same somehow; women holding the whip handle.

ANGELA	Don't knock it, dear, till you've tried it. Why are you really here, Violet? Had a row with hubby Cyril have we?

VIOLET	If you minded your own business as much as you mind other people's we'd all be the better for it.

ANGELA   I don't wonder you're on Little Boottox Council. That's a politician's answer. I'll ask again. Why are you here?

VIOLET   As I said, EU legislation. Just pretend I'm not here. *(Studies papers and at intervals roams around the clubhouse, opening doors and sniffing)*

ANGELA   Since when have you cowtowed to anyone?

LIONEL   We really must press on. Shower curtain I think.

DUDLEY   What about the replay of my match

LIONEL   Look, Dudley, we can't do everything. We've not even touched upon the *de*activation of the ladies' locker room keyhole.

ANGELA   *(Dramatically in Shakespearian tones)* To bung or not to bung, that is the question. I suggest we leave it as it is. It may solve the shortage of male members problem.

PRUDENCE   *(Writing in notepad)* Male members problem.

VIOLET   I didn't know we had a male members problem.

LIONEL   Leave the keyhole active then we may not have a male members problem. Is that carried unanimously? *(No response from committee)* I'd like to raise the issue of boxer shorts.

PRUDENCE   *(Writing)* Boxer shorts.

ANGELA   *(Nestles up to Lionel)* Now are we talking men's undies or boxing shorts?

LIONEL   Outer garments like what boxers wear.

ANGELA   *(Waning enthusiasm)* Oh.

PRUDENCE   *(Writing)* Boxing shorts.

NOREEN   Lionel says he'll stick with Y-fronts.

ANGELA   Thank you for sharing that nugget of information with us.

LIONEL   Honestly, Noreen, do keep some things private. We all know everybody else's business as it is.

PRUDENCE   Not everything.

ANGELA   *(Cooing with interest)* Oho.

PRUDENCE   You see you're not the fount of all wisdom you think you are.

ANGELA   Oho. Perhaps there's more to you than meets the eye.

DUDLEY   *(Offended)* And what's wrong with my pale blue boxing shorts?

LIONEL   *(Snorting)* Well in your summer house when you're knitting they're O.K. but not on club Saturday afternoon when we've a visiting team on the premises.

DUDLEY   Their number one took a fancy to them. Asked me where I'd bought them. Turned out to be a member of my knitting club.

LIONEL   I think we should stick to orthodox white men's shorts.

PRUDENCE   *(Writing)* Orthodox white men's shorts.

LIONEL   What shall we set down as the definition of orthodox white men's shorts.

ANGELA   *(Shakespearian tones)* To zip or not to zip, that is the question. I've been thinking.

PRUDENCE   Now there's a first.

ANGELA   *(Black look from Angela)* I'm not that keen on having a load of Little Boottox dignitaries prancing around our courts on Sunday afternoon.

LIONEL   It could do us some good locally. Prudence take down boxer shorts.

PRUDENCE   *(Writing)* Take down boxer shorts.

ANGELA   We see enough of those paperlifters during the week. Not on a Sunday I say.

LIONEL   *(Indignantly)* Hey, I say, I'm on the Little Buttox council.

YOU CAN'T BE SERIOUS

VIOLET   And so am I.

ANGELA   Who said that? *(Perking up)*   Anyway, trump card time, folks.

LIONEL   What's that?

ANGELA   *(Shouting)* Trump...card. *(Gets up. Takes leather jacket from back of her chair. Attempts to zip her jacket with difficulty over her bust. Teeters over to back of stage R where bar is. Takes from under bar shelf a bright red motorcycle helmet)* Just as soon as my 'phone call comes through I'm off out to meet someone young and *gorgeous* at the new wine bar. *(Looking at Noreen)* Knitting on the Chesterfield with Lionel and his Y-fronts is not my idea of life lived in the fast lane.

LIONEL   *(Alarmed)* But we're not half way through the meeting yet. We've still got shower curtain, teas, tournaments and A.O.B.

ANGELA   *(Teeters over to Lionel. Pets him. Flirts)* Lionel, sweetie, this lady's not for tempting, but I'll stay till my call comes through.

DUDLEY   Who is it? Is it anything I should know about?

ANGELA   That's my business. I'm going out.

DUDLEY   Out! Dressed like that at...

ANGELA   ...at my age? Is that what you were going to say? It's O.K. for you to go out, come out, be out, or whatever, but when it's a woman of a certain age, we ought to babysit our grandchildren, or *(Goes to the back of Noreen's chair. Puts her head near Noreen's ear)* go to the theatre with girlfriends who wouldn't know what sex was if you chucked it at them in *(Shouts over to Prudence)* binloads.

PRUDENCE   *(Writing)* Sex in binloads.

DUDLEY   *(Offended)* Sorry.

ANGELA   *(On a roll now. Walks behind table back to Dudley)* And they should put a health warning on human beings. The only way to survive family and friends is not to live near them. The human species is naturally warlike. Too much calm does their head in.

MARLON   *(Munching award winning chocolate cake)* My mother isn't warlike and I like living with my mother.

ANGELA   Yes, sweetie, but your girlfriends don't.

MARLON   *(Pouting)* They'd like her if they got to know her.

ANGELA   Well sweetie, you could say that about anyone. Who's going to wade through ten ton of doo-dah to find out if a person's nice?

MARLON   That does it. I'm only mowing once a week.

LIONEL   Look, Angela, can we please try to stick to the matter under discussion which is...which is...

ANGELA   Human nature.

LIONEL   Shower curtain.

MARLON   What we need a shower curtain for? If we didn't have that you could pay me to mow twice a week.

ANGELA   Why should the men have a new shower curtain when we've got an open keyhole? Fair dos. I've already dipped into our budget for that port-a-loo out on court five to accommodate members who can't make it back to the pavilion.

NOREEN   Pity you didn't dip a bit deeper and put a safe roof on.

ANGELA   *(Indignantly)* We forked out for a safety helmet.

LIONEL   I've never seen it. I want to know what my subscription is going on.

ANGELA   If it's not on the hook outside, *(Turning on Lionel)* it means someone's on the loo.

NOREEN   *(Puts her hand up)* Actually I've got it. I'm knitting a strap for it. We could run a jumble sale to pay for a shower curtain and a safe roof. I'd do the cakes.

ANGELA   *(Walking over to bar R)* Oh God. Give us a gin. Let's open this blooming bar.

(As one the committee arise, shove the committee table to L and stampede to the bar to place their orders)

VIOLET   I've just come to tell you that...no on second thoughts forget it.

ANGELA   Who said that?

VIOLET   Oh just pretend I'm not here.

ANGELA   You're up to something.

VIOLET   Of course not, dear *(Private smile)*

PRUDENCE   Do you think it's a good idea after what happened at the last meeting? You all got drunk; Noreen did the can-can on the table and *(To Angela who is behind bar counter)* getting you home was like shifting a beached whale.

ANGELA   *(Approaching Prudence aggressively)* You threw up in the waste paper bin and *(Lowers her head near Prudence's ear)* you'd only had a lemonade.

PRUDENCE   That was Dudley's winkle pate.

LIONEL   *(Snorting)* We all had that. It was like being in a Force Nine gale.

ANGELA   *(Walking across front of stage with a gin in her hand)* If there is a hell after this earthly life, it's the Great Wollop and Little Buttox members on the loose, rampaging towards Noreen's chocolate cake stall at the Little Boottox Jumble Sale on a wet Saturday afternoon and me *(Looking at glass)* without a gin in me hand. Oh and *(Honing in on Prudence)* a sanctimonious teetotaller on the committee. *(Returns to bar)*

DUDLEY   By the way, Ange, what's with the motorbike gear? Where's the passion wagon?

ANGELA   Rear suspension gone.

NOREEN   I'm not surprised.

LIONEL   Look can we stick to the agenda or we'll be here all night.

ANGELA   God forbid but I don't mind being at the bar all night. Let's let our hair down and bugger the agenda.

PRUDENCE   I thought you had a hot date to go to?

ANGELA   Well...uh...probably. *(Lonely look)*

NOREEN   Why do the men need a shower curtain? We haven't got one. Can I go in and inspect?

PRUDENCE   *(Writing)* Mrs Bumfrey went to the men's room.

(Exit Noreen with old-fashioned handbag stashed over arm, hands clasped defensively in front of her, through kitchen door which is also exit to clubhouse back door and changing room. As the evening progresses Noreen gets a little tipsy)

MARLON   Why didn't you pay *me* to put a safe roof on the privy?

ANGELA   You've never put a privy roof on in your life.

VIOLET   I want you round at my potting shed first thing tomorrow morning. I'll give you one more chance to get that handrail right.

ANGELA   Who said that?

MARLON   *(Waving a book at Angela)* I could get a book out of the library.

ANGELA   *(Bearing down on Marlon)* And I could get a book from the library on *DIY Strangulation*.

MARLON   *(Offended)* I can see what mother means about all mouth and big ti..

DUDLEY   Marlon!

NOREEN   *(Poking head round changing room door)* Well I vote we get a men's shower curtain. *(Indicating position of doors with hand movements)* The ladies' locker room door is right opposite the men's locker room door, and if they're both open at the same time, *(Pause)* well need I say more? *(Exit Noreen to locker rooms)*

PRUDENCE   *(Writing)* So we've decided to buy a shower curtain?

ANGELA   Spoilsports.

MARLON   If no-one's going to make a decision about paying me more I'm going home. I promised mother I'd put the kitchen cupboard up.

DUDLEY   Do we really need a shower curtain? Couldn't we pay Marlon for an extra mow instead?

PRUDENCE   *(Exasperatedly crossing out)* Oh!

ANGELA   *(Walking over to Marlon from the bar)* I'm almost tempted to open my handbag and pay for Marlon's extra mow and send him on a long holiday. Cheerful little soul, aren't you, Marlon. *(Pinches his cheek)*

NOREEN   *(Back at table after visit to bar. Drink in front of her. Getting tipsy)* I shudder to think what's in *your* handbag.

MARLON   Couldn't go abroad 'cos of me tubs.

DUDLEY   Your tubs?

MARLON   Me shrubs tubs need water regular.

ANGELA   Can't your mother do them?

MARLON   She don't like tubs.

DUDLEY   I'll do them.

MARLON   Then there's me decorating. I does me decorating in me 'olidays.

DUDLEY   I'm *not* doing your decorating. I come over all queer anywhere near a stepladder.

ANGELA   Oh the excitement of it all. *(Returns to bar, drink in hand)*

VIOLET   *(Draws Lionel away from bar and to front of stage. Angela earwigs)* Now, Lionel, I've been examining your match secretary expenses. This itemised 'phone bill. You seem to have been calling a lot of numbers beginning with 0891?

ANGELA   *(Angela walks over to talk into Noreen's ear)*
I knew itemised 'phone billing would be the death of turning a blind eye in marriage.

VIOLET   I've been doing some research because Cyril's been calling these numbers. He says it's financial advice so we'll be secure when we reach middle age. I 'phoned a few of the numbers and got Leatherclad Nuns, Miss Stern's Disciplinary Academy and some woman called Mrs Whippy.

LIONEL *(Noreen has had several drinks and is staring into space, sitting on a barstool)* Shush. Don't worry the wife about the telephone bill. Just a few wrong numbers. You know how it is. Oh and I was searching for an ice cream van for finals' day. No luck there. *(Lecherous snort)* Mrs Whippy said her husband was out.

VIOLET It's dubious, Lionel, very dubious. Remember as match secretary you *are* a figurehead for Little Boottox. We have a reputation to uphold. The club is not paying for these...um...wrong numbers. Now Noreen, in your capacity as club coach it is necessary I consult with you.

NOREEN My head's beginning to feel quite fuzzy. What was that Violet? You'd like to insult me? Well I don't mind. Lionel does it all the time.

LIONEL Noreen, concentrate.

VIOLET I will not have it.

DUDLEY What won't you have?

ANGELA More than once a year I expect.

VIOLET I heard that. That reminds me, Noreen have you got the tarts organised for tomorrow's ladies' match?

LIONEL *(Winking at Angela)* Look I've got a big agenda.

ANGELA *(Naughty giggle)* Hum.

DUDLEY Lionel's got a big agenda.

VIOLET We've all got big agendas.

ANGELA Isn't agenda already plural?

DUDLEY Oh Angela.

VIOLET I will not have frivolous abuse of the Club Suggestions Box.

DUDLEY What have the juniors - I assume it's juniors - written this time?

VIOLET   That the executive committee get one of their sailor friends to mend the net on Boottox End court.

DUDLEY   That's harmless enough. Nearly everyone in Little Buttox has sailor friends.

VIOLET   *(Studying some papers)* It's the rude and informative illustrations which bear a remarkable resemblance to members of our club.

DUDLEY   May one enquire as to what these people are doing and with whom?

(Angela's hand flies to her mouth)

VIOLET   I'd rather not. Noreen will you remonstrate with your juniors.

DUDLEY   Will you remonstrate with your juniors, Noreen?

NOREEN   *(Lifts head from bar counter)* Oh I don't coach them on that till their fourth year. Anyway what about my club juniors and coaching? We'll all be asleep by the time we get round to them.

ANGELA   Which one? The one who comes on Saturday, or the one who comes on Sunday?

NOREEN   I'm sure I'll get a group going once I'm certified.

ANGELA   Let's hope my legs will last till you get your coach's licence. Honestly, Noreen, I can't keep a place warm in Division five until you produce someone good enough for the team.

NOREEN   It's not my fault if they're slow learners and keep going off on adventure holidays for young offenders.

ANGELA   The last girl you sent to match practice couldn't even serve and she's been having coaching from you for two years.

NOREEN   *(Gets up)* Well the first year we do the forehand *(Demonstrates forehand)* the second year we do the backhand *(Demonstrates backhand)* and this year we're...(Begins to demonstrate the service and falls over at front of stage having knocked Marlon on the way, who has slid down in his chair with his cap over his head. Wailing)* Lionel.

LIONEL   *(Whilst rushing to help Noreen up and dragging to where he sits her on a chair)* Look, Ange, leave off my Nor will you? The kids are lucky to have someone of her experience.

DUDLEY   Darlings, we're all friends here and most of us are civilised human beings.

ANGELA   I'm not. I let my hang-ups hang out.

NOREEN   Both your hang-ups are disturbing to the human race.

LIONEL   Disrupting the lives of men who have reached the age of respectability and taking early retirement to spend more time with their families. *(Lionel dumps Noreen in her chair and sits down next to her. She keels over and flings her arms around Lionel's neck and asks Lionel)*

NOREEN   Do men ever reach the age of respectability?

ANGELA   Not the ones I know, thank goodness. I don't see why one should be expected to enter a sexual non-combat zone after thirty.

NOREEN   *(Waving a drink at Angela)* Or even forty.

DUDLEY   Awful to have a cut-off date.

ANGELA   I feel more now than I ever did when I was younger.

LIONEL   *(Lecherous snort)* Much more we hear.

ANGELA   Respectability suffocates fun. I can't think of a more terrible epitaph than 'She was a respectable woman.' It even sounds tight-arsed.

NOREEN   *Angela* do you have to?

ANGELA   Funny you only fluff your ears out when I talk dirty.

NOREEN   *(Waving gin)* Mrs Wayward-Gins.

PRUDENCE   What am I supposed to be taking down now?

ANGELA   *(Bearing down on Prudence)* And there's another poor soul'll have to warm her act up. Can't expect a man to prospect for forbidden - and well-hidden - treasure forever.

NOREEN   Do you enjoy being a bitch?

ANGELA That's rich coming from you.

PRUDENCE Can the club bring in a rule about kindness?

LIONEL Look we've had all this out at every committee meeting. Can't we put our foibles away for once and attend to my addendum? To summarise then. We've decided no boxing shorts on court.

ANGELA I'm all for that.

LIONEL Take that down, Prudence.

PRUDENCE *(Writing)* Take down boxer shorts.

LIONEL *(Clears throat)* Perhaps we can make a final decision on the shower curtain at our next meeting? It really is getting late. We've still got teas and tournaments to discuss. Noreen, I understand you're proposing that if any player does not offer acceptable refreshments, that regardless of playing standard, they cannot be considered for team selection?

ANGELA That rules me out.

DUDLEY Exactly. We may get more women's teams entering. Not everyone has a taste for your bile and spleen when losing.

ANGELA *(Wistful)* I've had some wonderful battles.

DUDLEY Singlehandedly you've depleted Division Five. There's only Little Buttox and Great Wollop left. All the other teams have refused to play you.

ANGELA *(Triumphantly)* So? We won didn't we? That's all that matters.

DUDLEY What matters is the taking part, and how you take part. When the totting up of our lives is done, it's not your achievements, but what sort of person you were.

PRUDENCE When am I going to be promoted from reserve?

ANGELA *(Walking over to Prudence. Hands on back of her chair)* As your Division Five captain it's up to me to decide when you're ready for it. You are obviously inexperienced in the battles of life i.e. tennis matches, so don't hold your breath, dearie.

PRUDENCE   *(Wails)*   How do I get experience when I'm never given any?

ANGELA   *(Walks to front of stage and straightens to her full majestic height)* You watch and you learn from experienced athletes - like me.

DUDLEY   God help us.

NOREEN   *(Raises her head from table)* I'll help you. I like to feel I'm making my contribution towards shaping the future generation.

ANGELA   Like Lionel did with your au pair?

NOREEN   As you say, Lionel and I make a good pair. We won the Mixed Handicap Veteran Doubles in...*(Shrugging)*...well it was in the last few years anyway. *(Whilst imbibing talks in confidential tones to Prudence)* You see, Prudence, persistence's the thing. If you want something badly enough, keep trying.

DUDLEY   Be trying, Prudence, like Noreen here.

NOREEN   I nearly gave up trying to find a life companion, but then God sent Lionel.

ANGELA   Not easy to place was our Noreen. For a long time you were unclaimed treasure, weren't you Noreen? *(Another slug of gin. Walks round table)* Mind you, don't you just wish some treasure would stay buried.

NOREEN   *(Bangs drink down on table)*   With a chest like yours it's no wonder no one gets close to you.

LIONEL   So what you're saying is have a decent bun in the oven or no selection?

NOREEN   Hear, hear. I know some round these parts who find it all too easy to get a bun in the oven.

ANGELA   And some round these parts have never ever reached Gas Regulo 6.

LIONEL   In order that the committees that come after us...

ANGELA   God help them.

LIONEL ...should have a definitive prototype to work from, don't you think we ought to record in precise detail in the minutes, exactly what constitutes a good tea? *(Bangs table)*

NOREEN Hear, hear.

LIONEL *(To Noreen)* Your department, I think, dear. I always like to consult experts in the field.

ANGELA Noreen's finest hour.

NOREEN *(Beginning to have difficulty with words)* Chocolate cake..

ANGELA Award winning

NOREEN ... sponge light as a feather with real cream and homemade strawberry jam cucumber sandwiches with cucumber cut just that thick *(Holds fingers to indicate thickness. Slurring)* and eggy-weggy schamdwiches with the crusts off best quality mayon... mayon... salad cream and proper tea out of a teapot and *not* that bloody urn.

DUDLEY Gracious. I'd die for a tea like that

ANGELA We nearly did after your last 'eggy-weggy' shamdwidges.

DUDLEY Well *some* eggs have salmonella.

ANGELA And *some* mayonnaise needs chucking out of the 'fridge after a year. *(Blowing on hands)* Why can't we have some heat on at these meetings? My hands are frozen.

LIONEL You can put them in my tracksuit pocket.

ANGELA *(Teeters seductively over to Lionel and puts her hand in his pocket. Both giggle and Angela flirts)* Oho lovely and warm. Don't minute that, Prudence.

NOREEN It's O.K. I doubt you'll get a better offer this evening. It's his new toy. Baby hot water bottle. I hope you didn't put boiling water in Lionel. I don't want it all perished by the time my dried flower evening in that draughty scout hut comes round. *(Head slumps on arms which are resting on bar counter)*

LIONEL I always read instructions meticulously.

(Committee groans)

ANGELA   Rattling good idea *I* think.

PRUDENCE   Where did you get it from? I could give one to Mummy for her birthday.

ANGELA   Whoopee. You and your bloody mother. Are you soldered together?

PRUDENCE   Anyway she's...

ANGELA   Mumsy? Cuddly? More dead than alive? When are you going to live a little?

PRUDENCE   That's a dreadful thing to say, especially...

ANGELA   I'm only pulling your leg.

PRUDENCE   You're cruel. You just trample on people's feelings without knowing any facts.

ANGELA   Oho?

PRUDENCE   Mind your own business.

ANGELA   Aren't we the dark horse, darling?

PRUDENCE   *(Fiercely)* Shut up.

ANGELA   Oho.

DUDLEY   Ladies, ladies, please. Now as a committed member, may I stick my oar in? Until we get heating organised, how about meeting at each other's houses on a rota system.

ANGELA   I don't feel I can say what I like if I'm not on neutral territory.

NOREEN   *(Raises head to look at Angela)* There are some people I wouldn't have in my potting shed, let alone my house.

ANGELA   I can't imagine you having anybody anywhere. *(Walks over to Noreen)* I doubt you'd make anybody's list of one hundred closest friends - *(Puts head next to Noreen's)* or should I say closet friends what with all these women's groups you go to?

NOREEN   You wouldn't know political correctness if you
bounced off it.

PRUDENCE   We can't have it at my place because mother goes to
bed at seven.

MARLON   Same here. We've a lot in common. My mother goes to bed at seven. She has lists. *(Ticking things off on a piece of paper)* 6 a.m. Get up; 6.30 a.m. Cup of tea; 7 a.m. Exercises.; 8.00 a.m. Marlon's sandwiches; *(Looking embarrassed)* 8.30 a.m. kiss Marlon goodbye; 9.00 a.m. open door for milkman; 9.30 a.m...

ANGELA   *(Standing imposingly centre stage)* ...Open door for milkman. Maybe she's not as daft as I thought. My mother opened the door for the milkman at 9.00 - evening that is - to let him out. *(Giggles)*

NOREEN   We couldn't have it at our place 'cos we like to finish the evening on a high note. *(Flings her arm across Lionel)* Sometimes we spread all over the floor and there's a real fight as to who can get the last piece of jigsaw in. *(Slumps head back onto arms)*

LIONEL   *(Looking at watch))* We've still got EU legislation to deal with. Though gawd knows what Brussels want with us now?

ANGELA   Only our souls.

PRUDENCE   *(Writing)* Aah .. *(Looking up)* souls?

LIONEL   *(Panicking)* What's this inspector going to be doing? What the hell are we going to do with him? I don't think our club practices will bear up to close scrutiny.

ANGELA   *(Has another drink.)* Open the bar; keep topping him up and *(Sensual voice as she teeters over to bar)* leave the rest to me.

LIONEL   *(Ignores)* This is where you come in, Marlon *(Hastily)* We'll pay you of course.

MARLON   *(Suspiciously)* Oh yeah?

LIONEL   We'll need a moat dug across the entrance to the club.

ANGELA   Are you expecting our advert in the *Little Boottox Gazette* to attract a stampede for membership?

MARLON   Why do we need a moat?

LIONEL Apparently Brussels want to eradicate diseases carried by foot.

DUDLEY We've all got to be dipped? How thrilling.

ANGELA And as chairman of the entertainments sub-committee, Dudley could do the baptising.

NOREEN *(Voice rising)* And what if I've got my best shoes on? What about when we're having our annual barn dance? We can't prance around all evening with wet feet.

LIONEL *(Peering at his papers)* Apparently you take your shoes off; dip the left sole first; then the right heel. They insist we construct a plastic platform 1.765 square metres in size.

ANGELA I can just see us all on a frosty morning, standing barefoot on our 1.765 square metre plastic platform. Do we have to dip all our souls?

PRUDENCE *(Writing)* Dip *(Looking up)* aah soles?

ANGELA Anyway, Noreen, simple, if you're worried about aah soles don't come to the barn dance.

NOREEN It's fun. We didn't all have to dance bosom to bosom like you and Violet 'cos there weren't enough men *(Rearing up from where she has been lying across two bar stools)* And when they tried to dance cheek to cheek they couldn't get within a hundred miles of each other. *(Hand movements indicating size of Angela and Violet's bosoms)* Boobies.

LIONEL *(Ignores)* Clause 14, sub-section 23: Teams from other counties have to be vetted with especial care, particularly Kent.

ANGELA Why Kent?

LIONEL It's obvious, darling. Channel Tunnel. Can't have all those foreigners traipsing in willy-nilly bringing in rabies and gawd-knows-what.

PRUDENCE What about tennis shoes? I carry an extra pair in my bag. Do I have to dip everything?

LIONEL *(Looks at papers)* Ah. Clause 8. Soiled plimsolls. Soiled plimsolls must be purified. *(Turns pages)*

ANGELA   Purified?

LIONEL   Yes, dear, derivative from purity. Hard for some of us to grasp.

ANGELA   *(Walks to lean seductively over Lionel's shoulder)* Oh do shut up. So how and when, Li, darling?

LIONEL   Every nine games like the ball change. Shoes off and thrown away. New pair out of the freezer.

NOREEN   Well I've never heard anything so daft. I'm not doing it. *(Bangs table in defiance)*

ANGELA   You'll be run out of town by the clipboard men. Actually I might enjoy that..hum.

DUDLEY   I'm with Noreen.

NOREEN   Good at least someone is. *(Lifts head from arms)* Are you? What happens to our mucky pumps?

ANGELA   Let me guess. They'll pay us subsidies to go barefoot and that will create plimsoll mountains all over the place.

MARLON   How much for the moat? I'm in demand you know. If we get plimsoll subsidies will you lower the subscription?

LIONEL   We'll probably have to raise subs because of having to create an *(Consults papers)* accredited storage area as a plimsoll disposal unit.

ANGELA   And where are we going to put our accredited storage area for a plimsoll disposal unit?

LIONEL   Obvious. Ladies' locker room.

ANGELA   I'm *not* changing next to a soiled plimsoll mountain.

NOREEN   I shudder at the very thought of a mountain of Lionel's used plimsolls.

LIONEL   Charming. I don't know why they're doing all this. Nobody's ever caught anything.

ANGELA   I suppose they're worried about plimsolly-transmitted diseases. Any way fiddle foot and mouth. I'd like to know what Brussels are going to do about global warming caused by flatulence in termites.

LIONEL   Hold on. I'll look that up. *(Thumbs through papers)*

DUDLEY   Get away? You're kidding. I'd have thought last Friday's curry tournament would have done more damage.

ANGELA   Scientific fact. Flatulence in termites. Heap big problem. Anyway if we're all going to be fried or frozen to death, I don't see why we should worry about plimsolly-transmitted diseases.

VIOLET   *(Clicks fingers)* Lionel, get my case, there's a dear. It's on our garden side of the ditch thanks to our groundsman's handy work.

LIONEL   Certainly. *(Exits through club entrance. Scurrying)*

VIOLET   *(Lionel returns with a suitcase. Members watch as Violet sticks notices on the board)*

ANGELA   We're not running those now. We're sticking to Pru's agenda and calling them Fondle Party and Pat and Punch Party.

VIOLET   You are not here to enjoy yourself. *(Picks up lavatory brush which Prudence put on a shelf)* What's been going on? I'm absolutely refuse to pay for another new lavatory brush. *(Peers through changing room and kitchen doors)*

ANGELA   *(Has another slug of drink)* Club rule number 69. Whilst on the premises of the Little Boottox Lawn Tennis Club thou shalt not enjoy thyself.

VIOLET   Don't be silly, Angela. You're club treasurer, you should be setting an example to these people. I think it's high time you women were in bed preparing for the match tomorrow. I'm on my way home right now. I like an early night before a match.

ANGELA   Poor Cyril. Actually we're in serious training. The balls get bigger after a few.

PRUDENCE   If you're all hung over, can I have a Great Wollop team place?

ANGELA *(Bearing down on Prudence)* No chance, baby. Rule Number 70 of the club rules. All team members must have undertaken bar training. Hollow legs required.

LIONEL Order, order. Members, please, aren't we going off at a tangent?

NOREEN Where were we? Mine's a gin.

DUDLEY Tournaments?

ANGELA Men's shower curtain? Why are seventy-five per cent of club committee meetings about shower curtains and it's always the men's?

LIONEL Drains, I think. Oh we put those off, didn't we?

NOREEN Junior coaching?

LIONEL We never stuck to the chewing gum issue? Mine's a pint, big Ange.

MARLON *(Puts down his pint)* Would you come with me to the Pat and Punch Party, Prudence?

PRUDENCE *(Nervously)* I'll have to let you know, Marlon.

MARLON *(Looks miserable)*

ANGELA *(Walks over to Prudence, drink in hand)* You're learning. Make 'em work for it. Now whenever I'm asked out...

LIONEL Thank you, Angela

VIOLET *(Drops a drawing pin. Loud scream as she bends to pick it up. En masse the committee rush to assist)* I'll have to lie flat. *(Committee amid much grunting and groaning manoeuvre her into a lying flat on her back position. She is in front of the committee table where the audience can see her. Reminiscent of a beached whale)* Ring Cyril. He's the only one who knows how to handle me.

ANGELA No one else would want to.

VIOLET Some of us come under exclusive labels. My mobile's in my case.

(Lionel opens her suitcase. Pile of interesting things are transferred onto the committee table before he finds the mobile i.e. horse harness, riding whip, colander, etc)

ANGELA *(Hums with interest at the accoutrements that pile onto the table)* Looks like they don't call the villages round here Little Boottox and Great Wollop for nothing. I wonder what she does with the colander?

LIONEL Shall I ring for you?

VIOLET Do dear boy. *(Lionel presses the digits she calls out to him and hands phone to Violet. In voice of authority)* Cyril. Your little chicken here. Be an angel and bring the trailer round. Me back's gorn. I'll need a ride. No I can't get home across the plank. Put down whatever you're messing with and come at once. *(Puts 'phone down. To committee members.)* Pretend I'm not here.

LIONEL *(Clears throat)* Right. Tournaments. Do we really want handicap events?

ANGELA You won't get the Reginald Barrington-Wotsits saying all our club members were born equal. They won't accept people in trade.

NOREEN They let you in.

ANGELA I passed my playing in test with flying colours. Be grateful you joined so long ago they didn't have tests. With your standard of tennis, you'd still be retaking yours.

PRUDENCE *(Brightly)* Is that a yes to handicap tournaments?

NOREEN Lionel and me'll enter. I'll do the catering.

PRUDENCE *(Murmurs as writing)* Cakes by Noreen.

ANGELA Noreen, By Royal Appointment, please. When you think who she supplies.

NOREEN *(Simpering)* I am allowed to say the Barrington-Oojimiflips come to me for all their private functions.

PRUDENCE Don't you think that's an elitist view of trade?

ANGELA	Wow. Dissent in the young. I love it. Come on, dear, be a rebel. Too many young women still believe Mr Right is lurking somewhere and will roll up in his four-wheel drive Discovery to discover what no-one else has discovered.

PRUDENCE	I think I'm about to be discovered.

LIONEL	I'm not free to be discovered.

ANGELA	*(Black look at Noreen)* Don't we know it.

LIONEL	What about *Spitzenfahrt*?

NOREEN	I schtill don't understand what all this spitting and farting is all about?

ANGELA	Little Boottox is twinned with *Spitzenfahrt*. It's a sort of Anglo-German Nooky Exhange. Rules you and Prudence out of course.

LIONEL	We're not having any of that. It's a serious match?

ANGELA	The last time you men had a serious match you dressed up in women's clothing.

LIONEL	That was for charity.

ANGELA	*(Walking to bar for another drink)* Oh yeah? I expect you took them to Nightingales.

LIONEL	Nightingales?

NOREEN	I expect it's something nasty.

LIONEL	Hum?

DUDLEY	*(Hand gesticulation towards Violet)* I'm not playing if I have to have Violet's Cyril as a partner.

VIOLET	*(Ouch)* Pretend I'm not here.

UNISON	*(Committee members ask each other)* Who said that?

ANGELA	I know as a club we've a reputation for playing with anybody but I'm not playing with Violet.

VIOLET   That's probably the only sensible thing you've said all night. Not a good idea to mix the classes.

ANGELA   Just wait till I play you in the next veterans' tournament. We'll see about class.

LIONEL   It'll be a blood bath.

PRUDENCE   None of us speaks any German.

ANGELA   *(Walking over to Prudence, drink in her hand. Puts head close)* Be guttural, darling. Sound as though you're being sick and cover them with spit. It got me through as a reporter in Germany.

PRUDENCE   If Violet's back's not better, can I have a Great Wollop... team place?

VIOLET   Talk about dead women's plimsolls. You're not experienced enough to fill mine yet.

ANGELA   What with plimsolly-transmitted diseases, I doubt Brussels would allow it, darling. Anyway, Noreen's playing.

PRUDENCE   I thought *I* was reserve?

ANGELA   You're second reserve. Noreen's bringing a prune tart.

PRUDENCE   *(Goes into broom cupboard/clothes hanging room R)* You lot discriminate against youth.

ANGELA   Hum. Stroppy.

NOREEN   When it comes to baking and club matches there's no substitute for ex...whatever.

LIONEL   *(Calling to Prudence)* Ladies please. It's getting late. Prudence can I trouble you for the minutes for Thursday?

PRUDENCE   Oh I won't be able to read that lot back. You know what my shorthand's like?

ANGELA   *(Nodding towards broom cupboard)* Terrible shorthand.

PRUDENCE *(Shouting from broom cupboard)* So what have we decided? *(Committee look at each other bemused and there are a few murmurs like 'what have we decided?' Prudence emerges from broom cupboard dressed in black leather trousers, white leather jacket, carrying a motorcycle helmet. Does a twirl, opening her jacket and showing revealing decolletage glittering top showing cleavage)* Anyway got to go now.

DUDLEY You look nice, Prudence.

PRUDENCE Thank you, Dudley. I've turning over a new leaf and going mod.

ANGELA *(Little girl voice)* Mummy waiting up? Worried about her little baby?

PRUDENCE *(Proudly)* No. I'm meeting Timothy at the new wine bar. His new year's resolution is to play more *mixed* doubles, Dudley *(Looks at Dudley)* in the *(Walks meaningfully over to Angela)* younger age groups, Angela, *dear.* *(Stunned looks on faces of Dudley and Angela)* 'Bye. *(Exits quickly out of club entrance centre back stage)*

MARLON I thought...*(Walks towards the audience, his face a picture of misery)*

ANGELA Well you little minx. Did you hear what she said to me. *(Walks to door. Lionel rushes after her to stop her going out. She opens door. Door partially open. Door handle comes off in Angela's hand)*

NOREEN I think it'll need a screw.

LIONEL Not now dear.

(Chuckle from Violet on floor. Sound of voices from near club entrance)

PRUDENCE *(Off) (Loudly)* Oh Hello. Can I help you?

VOICE *(Off) (Foreign Accent)* I am Hans Groppen, Head of Club Legislation in Brussels.

(Committee are frozen in positions)

PRUDENCE *(Off) (Loudly)* Oh, well actually I'm just going but the rest of the committee are in there, why don't you go in and have a drink, you couldn't have come at a better time.

VOICE   *(Off) (Shouting)* A drink ? I hope you are avare of the new EU legislation...no alcohol consumption on club premises. Anyone found drinking on club premises will be prosecuted and the club may be closed down. So, you are a Little Buttox committee member?

PRUDENCE   *(Off)* Yes.

VOICE   *(Off)* Your Brussels representative in Little Buttox told your vice president, Mrs Violet Lissom-Green about the alcohol rule. Did she not inform you?

ANGELA   *(Hissing to Violet)* You traitor.

PRUDENCE   *(Off)* No. I don't even know who our Brussels representative is.

VOICE   *(Off)* Who should I address myself to in there?

PRUDENCE   *(Off) (Quickly)* Oh I recommend you address yourself to our club treasurer, *Mrs Wayward-Jones*; she's very Europe orientated ... *she'll* take care of you.

(Footsteps recede on gravel. Motorbike roars off. Silence. Various reactions of panic from the committee. Knock at front door L Animal-like stampede at high speed through kitchen door, off stage and through the auditorium R, using both aisles. Violet left lying on floor. The bar is open. There are glasses and bottles everywhere and she cannot move because of her back. Last member to disappear through kitchen door is Angela)

VIOLET   Look here you chaps, what about me?

(As a parting gesture to a friend, Angela rushes back and places a bottle in Violet's hand, then hightails it through kitchen door after the others)

ANGELA   Bugger you.

CURTAIN

INTERVAL

(Tennis Club bar open. People playing short tennis over net with soft balls on green baize in front of curtain. Tennis music playing)

ACT II

SCENE 1

(During the interval tennis music is playing. It is early summer. Whole theatre becomes a tournament ground. During the interval two of the production company have been playing short tennis over the net on green baize situated below front stage. Younger members of audience encouraged to join in. The draw of the Great Wollop veterans' tournament contains an ominously large entry of competitors from the notorious Little Buttox Tennis Club. Several deck-chairs and garden chairs are grouped around the umpire chair. A sleeping Lionel in tennis attire and white cap lies in a deck-chair with legs propped up on garden chair L A knitting Noreen sits R of centre back stage umpire chair. Sports bags and tennis paraphernalia litter the ground. An oxygen tank is L of umpire chair. Sounds of tennis matches in progress with the odd 'you can't be serious'. Far R is referee's office. Clouded glass so cannot see in. When referee's office is being used, silhouettes of referee and competitors can be seen. Enter Angela through auditorium L of umpire chair with tennis racket. Dressed in tennis skirt and revealing white tennis top. To save employing an extra actor, Cattermole, the referee is played in silhouette and the voice supplied by a member of the production company)

(See Ground Plan)

ANGELA   I need a blow. Got a tissue, Lionel, darling? I think my knicker elastic's about to give up the ghost too. *(Back to audience as she worriedly checks her knicker elastic and bends down to rummage in sports bag by umpire stand. White knickers with black imprint of a hand on each buttock)* Got a safety pin?

LIONEL   *(Splutters awake)* Uhh, uhh, what?

NOREEN   *(Not looking up from knitting)* Your knickers are an act of trust. I'd have thought with your experience, you'd include tissues and an extra pair when you pack your sports bag. Actually I'm surprised you've got any knickers on at all. You didn't last time.

ANGELA   *(To Noreen)* We're not all efficient like you and pack four pairs of flannelette knickers *(To Lionel)* with reinforced gussets.

LIONEL   *(Shielding eyes from sun with arm)*   Who are you playing, Ange?

ANGELA   That doyenne of Little Boottox society, Lady Violet.

Did you know she used to keep a menstrual chart of all her opponents so she'd know when they were having an off day?

LIONEL (*Lecherous snort*) Don't you mean an 'on' day?

ANGELA (*Sits L of umpire stand next to oxygen tank*)

NOREEN Shows your age that she no longer does where you're concerned.

ANGELA Shows your standard that she never did where you're concerned.

DUDLEY (*Enter Dudley through auditorium L*) Whew. (*Sits down R of umpire chair and mops his brow*) Not like our days at Bognor when we could play all day and live it up all night. Got any energy pills, Lionel?

LIONEL (*Asleep again*)

NOREEN He's brings everything. Judging by your score what you need are jump leads. Your Bognor days are long gone, but the repercussions reverberate on.

ANGELA (*Towelling down*) Do you know something, Noreen, your tongue ought to be wheel clamped. (*Hits her arm*) Gawd. What's that? World War 2 torpedo? (*Giggles*) I'd like to see the size of the batteries that go in that.

NOREEN And they've got closed circuit television when you're playing.

DUDLEY (*Jumping up and down and practising tennis strokes*) EU regulations, my darling. Oxygen tanks compulsory at all over forty events.

ANGELA You can't be serious? What about my street cred? If my umpire stand's got a torpedo strapped to its leg, they'll know I'm over forty. Any chance of a quick whiff before Violet gets back. It could be the answer to my prayers. (*Draws in oxygen from mask attached to oxygen tank*) That's better. I'm going to report Violet to the LTA for violation of loo rolls (*Giggles*) sorry, loo rules. She's gone off for another loo break and we've only played three games.

DUDLEY   Do you think she's breaking Great Wollop tournament rules and consulting a coach?

NOREEN   She can't be. I'm the coach.

ANGELA   *(Busy refurbishing herself sartorially at umpire stand)* I think Dudley meant a proper coach.

NOREEN   The trouble with you Angela is that you're so obsessed with yourself you can't appreciate real talent when you see it.

ANGELA   *(Spraying deodorant under armpits)* Talent. Huhh. Mind you I did ask you to give Violet a serve that would put her back out and it did.

NOREEN   Don't be silly. She did that getting into the Robin Reliant when Cyril impounded her Jag.

ANGELA   *(Spraying deodorant on legs)* Hmm interesting. Cyril only takes the Jag away when Violet's up to naughties. I wonder who with. I must find out when she's going to do something else that Cyril would like to know about? I might be able to use it to my advantage.

NOREEN   You're a disgusting, egotistical, opportunistic bitch, Angela.

ANGELA   *(Sprays deodorant up skirt)* Yeah, good fun isn't it?

DUDLEY   Are you winning, Angela?

ANGELA   Haven't a clue. Violet's had three loo breaks and no service breaks.

DUDLEY   One must exercise patience when playing Violet. I've had her in the mixed doubles.

ANGELA   Lucky you. Who's refereeing this wrinklies' tournament?

DUDLEY   Cattermole.

NOREEN   We need someone like him to keep you in order, Angela.

ANGELA   I'll soon sort him out.

NOREEN   Don't be too sure. Some people are mild-mannered until they get behind the wheel of a car. The same can apply to referees. Put some people behind a referee's desk and you've got Machiavelli and a wolf in tennis player's clothing all rolled into one.

ANGELA   Wait and see.

NOREEN   He's a pig of a man.

ANGELA   Heard about Achilles' heel?

DUDLEY   I don't know where I'm going to find the energy for the Pat and Punch Party tonight. You going Ange?

ANGELA   I doubt it.

DUDLEY   *(Disappointed)* I want a quickie match 'cos of the Pat and Party

ANGELA   Since Pru's agenda, no one calls them Pate and Punch Parties anymore. Prudence joining us?

DUDLEY   You can't expect a young person like her to want to watch an old crocks' tournament.

NOREEN   You must miss not having her around. No-one to sharpen your tongue on Angela?

ANGELA   It's a mite boring without her.

NOREEN   I'm surprised to want her company. You've nothing in common.

ANGELA   A love of tennis is a good common denominator for anyone.

NOREEN   Then let her into the team.

ANGELA   Then I'd have to chuck an old bag like you out.

NOREEN   You're so immature.

DUDLEY   Ladies. Ladies.

ANGELA *(Smooths tennis skirt down)* I've got to go. Mustn't keep our president of vice waiting. *(Exit Angela and Dudley L through auditorium. Large raspberry sound. Angela and Dudley reappear with startled look on faces then exit)*

NOREEN You can't blame the dog this time.

LIONEL Well it wasn't me. *(Argument starts. Angela and Violet are on different sides of the auditorium. Their voices emanate from different sides of auditorium, simulating a tennis match with ball being bashed back and forth. Audience heads flick from right to left as in a tennis match as they watch the two women in action)*

ANGELA *(Approaching from back of auditorium to ultimately enter L)* I suppose you're going to call that out too, Violet *dear*?

VIOLET *(Approaching from back of auditorium to enter R)* It *was* out.

ANGELA *(Auditorium left)* It was in. My game.

VIOLET *(Auditorium right)* And you're footfaulting.

ANGELA *(Auditorium left)* So are you, but as you can never get within a hundred miles of the net, it doesn't matter. Anyway at Great Wollop only an umpire or linesman can call footfaults.

VIOLET *(Auditorium right)* They couldn't get anyone to umpire our match.

ANGELA *(Auditorium left)* I'm not surprised. You dragged the last one off his chair. If you had a decent backhand you wouldn't need to cheat. Noreen's creation I suppose.

NOREEN *(Knitting)* Charming.

VIOLET *(Auditorium right)* That's it. I'm getting the referee.

ANGELA *(Auditorium left)* Won't do you any good. He's probably got an understanding with someone else now.

VIOLET *(Auditorium right)* You cow.

ANGELA Hell hath no fury like a veteran tennis player losing to someone younger. How do you know it's not me he's got an understanding with?

VIOLET *(Auditorium right. Mounts steps to enter R. Shouting)* After Bognor nothing would surprise me. Referee. *(Enters referee's office where she can be seen in silhouette, remonstrating with Cattermole)*

(Enter Angela L to umpire chair. Tennis balls stuck up each back side of frillies. Dabbing nose with hankerchief. Swinging tennis racket)

ANGELA She's getting the referee. All I said was, I suppose you're going to call that out?

LIONEL You certainly have a way with words, Ange.

NOREEN You can always be relied upon to say the right word at the right time to upset the right person. Poor old Violet. Is she with Cattermole? *(Pronounced Ca-er-maul)*

(Lionel and Angela correct her) Ker-ter-mer-lay. *(Expellation of air)*

NOREEN It wasn't me.

ANGELA That's surprising. You look as though you live on stewed prunes.

(Sitting L of umpire stand. Angela still using deodorant. Enter Dudley)

DUDLEY I'm completely puffless. What's cooking? I've just seen Violet storming into the referee's office and all the matches have stopped.

(Loudspeaker system comes on a full blast)

CATTERMOLE *(Silhouette of Cattermole sitting down in referee's office and Violet holding a tennis racket over his head can be seen)* Hello my little fluffy bunnykins.

VIOLET I'll give you fluffy bunnykins. You're not seeing that cow, Angela, are you? You've not taken her to Bognor Beach have you?

CATTERMOLE Of course not. Now come here and give Mr Bunnykins a big cuddle.

VIOLET I don't know why not. With her backside she wouldn't feel the pebbles. If I find out you've been seeing that tart, you'll be walking funny for a week.

ANGELA (*Leaping from her chair*) How dare she. (*Storming into referee's office*) How dare you broadcast aspersions about me.

CATTERMOLE Oh hello dear.

ANGELA Do you realise the whole ground has heard every word?

CATTERMOLE Oh no. (*Fumbling with switches*) Oh God how does this thing go off.

ANGELA Oh no you don't (*Elbows Cattermole and Violet aside. Grabs microphone. Speaks into it. Profile of her bust can be seen. Change to a softer more seductive voice*) Ladies and gentlemen, can I have your attention please? If any competitor fancies a good bonk at Bognor Beach, please sign the form at the referee's table. Also, if you would like to enter the mixed age handicap doubles, the referee is now short of female competitors, as Violet Lissom-Green and myself are about to deal with a pairing problem which has arisen due to an error in selection. Finally, (*Hard, meaningful note in voice*) secondhand balls are available from the referee at squashed down prices. (*Snort from Lionel*) Thank you ladies and gentlemen. You may resume your matches. Thank you. (*Angela hurls microphone on desk. Violet slaps referee's face and marches out across back of stage, to L of umpire chair. Angela trots behind. Joins Violet at umpire stand. They are obviously arguing*)

CATTERMOLE (*Picks up microphone*) I'm most awfully sorry, ladies and gentlemen, but we appear to have a stray transmission from a Radio Bognor play. Will you please resume your matches without further delay.

ANGELA (*To Violet*) If you think I'm going to be on the same court, let alone planet, as you after that sullying of my reputation, you've got another think coming.

DUDLEY (*Peels a banana*)

VIOLET Look my dear, let's be adult about this. If we don't play we'll be chucked out of our draws. Anyway have you got a reputation to sully?

ANGELA How do you know it wasn't your Cyril I sullied with?

VIOLET Too ridiculous. Cyril's got impeccable taste.

ANGELA What's taste got to do with it?

NOREEN   You two have got staying in your draws - tournament draws that is - down to a fine art.

ANGELA   *(To Noreen)* Shut up. *(To Violet)* I don't care if we are chucked out of our draws.

VIOLET   Of course you care. If we pull out now, we'll be letting down the reputation of Little Boottox Tennis Club.

NOREEN   Bit late to worry about that.

ANGELA   On second thoughts, Cattermole's not worth missing a tennis match over.

VIOLET   Precisely. Anyway tennis is more exciting than sex.

DUDLEY   *(Dudley bites into his banana)*

ANGELA   Well I suppose you would know, fluffy bunnykins.

VIOLET   Dudley don't you ever do anything other than knitting and decapitating bananas?

DUDLEY   Nutrition for serious tennis players.

VIOLET   Your serve, Angela dear, roller end. *(Turns to exit, followed by Angela. Lionel interrupts)*

LIONEL   By the way, Violet *dear,* before you go it wouldn't have been you who got Herr Groppen to call at an inappropriate time during that committee meeting?

VIOLET   You mean whilst you were all in a disgusting state? Now why on earth would I want to do that? I'm your vice president? Anyway I would hardly have arranged for Herr Groppen to call whilst I was on the premises?

ANGELA   Ahh but you'd only come to stick a few notices up. If your back hadn't 'gorn' you'd have been gone long before Mr Groping arrived.

LIONEL Oh and another thing, Violet, I hear your uuh friend, Cattermole, is looking for a defunct tennis club to buy up so he can start up his own sports club? Handy for him if Brussels closed us down? It'll put my Noreen out of business and he can run his ladies' coffee morning coaching orgies without any competition from unique coaches like my Noreen.

ANGELA Oh and another thing, Violet, isn't your Cyril looking for a languishing tennis club as a business investment and lo and behold you get what you've always wanted; ladies' tennis captain of the new Little Boottox Sports Club. *(Picking up tennis balls)* Fortunately we Little Boottox members think on our feet. So noble of you, Violet, to sacrifice yourself for the club. As you were the only one drinking at the club on that night, you're the only one who gets prosecuted.

VIOLET Bad luck, Angela, I'm not going to be prosecuted. I told the official we were amalgamating with the Little Boottox Thespian Society on a play, had just finished rehearsing and the bottles and glasses were all props.

ANGELA And he believed you? Pull the other one.

VIOLET I have contacts in high places.

ANGELA More like you're having an understanding with our Brussels representative in Little Boottox and he got you off.

NOREEN The person who got her off was Cattermole. He's our representative.

ANGELA How did you know that?

NOREEN Mrs Floggitt at the village stores told the milkman, the milkman told Marlon's mum, Marlon's mum told Marlon, Marlon told Lionel and Lionel told me. All in the strictest confidence of course.

ANGELA *(To Violet)* And why didn't you tell us about the no alcohol rule?

VIOLET I forgot.

ANGELA Oh yeah?

VIOLET You chaps *(Pronounced 'cheps')* have a vivid imagination. I'm too awf'ly fond of Little Boottox.

ANGELA	The whole thing sounds like pigs' snouts in troughs. If you knew what I know about Cattermole you wouldn't be able to concentrate on our *(Mimicking Violet)* 'metch.'

VIOLET	I expect you know him as well as anyone after pairing with him in all those Bognor tournaments. Oh come on let's get on with the match. *(Pronounced 'metch')* A woman of my standing has many engagements to get to. Your serve, dear, roller end.

ANGELA	You've just said that. No wonder you can never remember the score.

VIOLET	I score after every point.

ANGELA	Don't we just know it. Come on, fluffy bunnykins.

(Exit Angela and Violet)

NOREEN	The secretary of my women's group called tennis players flat, flippant, one-dimensional and full of middle-class prejudices.

LIONEL	*(Sitting on chair L of umpire stand by oxygen tank)* I wouldn't call Angela and Violet flat. *(Lecherous snort. Lionel leans on tank. Dozes off. Sound of tennis balls. Noreen knitting. Huge raspberry, followed by a crash. Oxygen tanks falls over with a bang. Lionel falls off chair. Enter Angela)*

ANGELA	Gawd. What was that?

(Enter Dudley)

DUDLEY	I knew the curry tournament was a mistake.

NOREEN	Lionel, speak to me.

LIONEL	*(On ground)* I'm O.K. Was it a bomb or are you losing, Ange?

ANGELA	Ha ha. It's the torpedo. Look. It's gorn 'orf. *(Leg propped up on chair. Towelling down)*

LIONEL	It's supposed to save lives. It nearly gave me a heart attack.

VIOLET	*(Enter Violet through auditorium to appear L.)* I'm fetching the groundsman.

ANGELA Why don't you fetch Mr Bunnykins?

DUDLEY Ange, shut it. We've just been torpedoed. Just for once can't we all be friends?

VIOLET I'll rake the groundsman from his hut. I don't know how we athletes can concentrate on the job, with all these exploding court accessories hanging around. Bloody Brussels. *(Bellowing as she exits)* Groundsman, groundsman. *(Exit Violet L through auditorium)*

ANGELA *(Rubbing lower leg)* I've pulled something.

LIONEL Perhaps I can help? I've done a massage course. I've got quite a large curriculum now.

ANGELA *(Nods head. Lionel manipulates her lower leg)* I'm surprised you let him do it Noreen.

NOREEN He'd only be doing something else.

ANGELA What else is there?

DUDLEY Oh no.

ANGELA *(Looking R)* No.

LIONEL *(Looking R)* No.

NOREEN God he's not groundsman here as well?

(Enter Marlon R Length of toilet roll hanging out of pocket. Cap on back to front. Screwdriver. Goes to umpire chair to enact a repair)

LIONEL Didn't know you worked here?

MARLON *(Shakes screwdriver at them)* If you paid me more I wouldn't have to. Is Prudence here?

(Enter Violet through auditorium L.)

VIOLET There you are, my good man, now remove this thing?

MARLON Nope.

VIOLET Nope? What do you mean, 'nope?' Do you have to screw while I'm talking to you?

MARLON   *(Carries on screwing)* Memo from Brussels last week. Only licensed handlers can touch 'em.

ANGELA   That's O.K. then. Violet's a *(Rural accent)* licensed handler.

MARLON   *(Bending to speak to Dudley who is sitting L of umpire stand)* I could have sworn it was you Friday evening careering down Privet Row in black leather with Angela on the back riding sidesaddle? *(Anxiously)* It wasn't Prudence and Timothy?

LIONEL   Couldn't have been Angela because we were sorting out our club draws. There that's a good rub.

NOREEN   You never do that for me.

ANGELA   *(Ignores)* If it had been us, *I* would have been in the driving seat.

DUDLEY   My bosses accept a lot of things but not me dressed in black leather.

ANGELA   You never know, you might get promotion. Anyway, Marlon, don't change the subject. If you don't move these oxygen tanks at once, I'm round at your Mum's to tell her I saw you in a sleazy club in Bognor last Saturday night.

MARLON   Looks like I'll have to break regulations and move it.

DUDLEY   Hold on. If you saw Marlon what was our Division Five ladies' captain doing at a sleazy club in Bognor?

ANGELA   Counselling fallen women. Talking of fallen women, look who's here.

                (Enter Prudence in summer dress)

PRUDENCE   *(Looking rather coy)* Hello everybody.

        (Angela raises her eyes to the heavens. Prudence sits down)

MARLON   *(Pointing to oxygen tank)* What do you lot want me to do with this?

VIOLET   You've just told us you can't handle it.

MARLON	It 'ud be more than my job's worth. I'm under the doctor as it is.
VIOLET	*(Black look at Angela)* Let the referee handle it. He's handled nearly everything else.
MARLON	*(Walks over to where Prudence is sitting. Bends his head down to be level with her)* I'm going bird spotting on Saturday. Would you like to come with me? Mother says you can come back for tea and madeira cake afterwards?
ANGELA	If you'd said award-winning chocolate cake I couldn't be responsible for my actions.
PRUDENCE	*(Embarrassed)* I'm sorry, Marlon, I can't, because Timothy's changing my plugs.
ANGELA	As long as he's not greasing your...
NOREEN	Angela.
MARLON	*(Sadly)* Another time may be.
PRUDENCE	Will you thank your mother for me?
VIOLET	*(Irritably)* Look, Marlon, must you stand there fiddling? Come with me. I'll show you how to handle referees. *(Exit Violet and Marlon. Grabs Marlon's hand and drags him off stage)*
ANGELA	*(Calls after them)* You'll be in good hands; she's handled a few in her time.
MARLON	*(Reappears)* If they paid me more...Honestly my mother's not well...I'm under the doctor as it is...*(Violet drags him off through auditorium)*
OPPONENT	*(Off)* If you're not back on court to finish our match right now, I'm fetching the referee.
DUDLEY	Excuse me, folks, but I'm surrounded by exploding tanks. I don't know how I'm expected to concentrate. *(Exit Dudley)*
ANGELA	*(To Prudence)* What have you been up to. You look exhausted.
PRUDENCE	Motor cycle maintenance. I'm teaching Timothy.

ANGELA   How sweet. And what, pray, is he teaching you?

PRUDENCE   About life.

ANGELA   I could tell you about that.

PRUDENCE   Thank you but I don't want to end up like you.

ANGELA   *(Looks hurt. Picks up some balls)* He'll dump you. You'll get hurt.

PRUDENCE   Why would you care about that?

ANGELA   *(Puzzled)* I don't know.

PRUDENCE   You hope I get hurt because of the way the committee meeting ended. Just for once I won.

ANGELA   I'm experienced at getting hurt. Balls...aah there they are. Oh well back to Violet. See you later.

(Exit Angela. Noreen knits then takes off tennis shoes and sits in her sock-clad feet. Lionel sleeps)

NOREEN   We ought to think about getting ready. We might be on for our match at any moment.

LIONEL   *(Lionel splutters intermittently then wakes from snooze.)* Are we back at Bognor?

NOREEN   *(Not looking up from knitting)* You seem to have a fixation about Bognor.

LIONEL   Had one of my greatest triumphs there once. A young chap can get a lot of experience at the Bognor tournament.

NOREEN   You're a nutcase. Prudence if you want to know how to win tennis matches without actually playing good tennis watch Angela and Dudley.

(Sounds of tennis balls being hit back and forth)

PRUDENCE   *(Sits in chair next to Noreen)* Do you mind if I ask you a personal question? You and Lionel seem to get on well?

NOREEN   *(Pauses in knitting. Looks at matches)* I can't imagine how you could think that?

PRUDENCE   I mean you're always together and...

NOREEN   ...arguing. Some people stay together because being alone seems worse or they know no-one else will have 'em.

PRUDENCE   But you're always together.

NOREEN   *(Knitting more slowly)* There must be exceptions I suppose, but early passion doesn't sustain you through those weary years of middle age; maybe shared hobbies do? *(Stops knitting. Looks into distance. Shrugs. Looks at her knitting again)* I don't know.

PRUDENCE   Did you know early passion?

NOREEN   *(Looks at Lionel asleep in chair, head back, mouth open. He gives a couple of great snorts)* I can't remember. It gets all fogged up. I sometimes think I'd like to feel like that again and then I can't remember how it is I'd like to feel. *(Noreen gets elasticated bandages from her sportsbags and puts them on her knees)*

PRUDENCE   *(Wistfully)* Relationships just don't seem to work nowadays. They don't seem to for me anyhow. With my background I always seem to eventually screw them up. I'd like what you've got only no one I know wants to settle down.

NOREEN   Most people do eventually. Have to. Their legs run out of steam, *(Looks at Lionel)* as do other *accoutrements*.

PRUDENCE   I don't have that sort of time. It's all right for men. Although all things considered, I don't know if I want children.

NOREEN   Children aren't everything, my dear. We don't see our lad from one end of the year to the other. He's busy with his job and his relationships. We might as well not be his parents. Stay single and enjoy yourself. *(Pats Prudence's hand)* That's my advice.

PRUDENCE   But you seem so together?

NOREEN   We argue from morning till night and the only thing we seem to agree on, is taking the opposite view. Do you call that together?

PRUDENCE   But don't people only fight about things and people they care about?

NOREEN   You could be right, dear. The only thing I'm certain about is that when we get home tonight he'll tell me over his malted milk how many volleys I missed, how I could have been better; and one of us will be sleeping with the dog.

PRUDENCE   I think we're in the middle of a social revolution. Do you think so?

NOREEN   My women's group think so, but then they're either single or living with someone. They think I'm a dinosaur. You're not from round here, dear, are you?

PRUDENCE   I was born in Bognor.

NOREEN   Angela's from Bognor. Well I don't know if she was born there. I can't imagine Angela being *born* anywhere. More like visiting from another planet.

PRUDENCE   I can't stand her. She seems to haunt me.

NOREEN   Yea like our wood rot.

LIONEL   *(Waking)* Is it macaroni cheese tonight?

NOREEN   I don't think I'm socially revolting yet and I'll give you one guess as to who'll be cooking the macaroni cheese.

LIONEL   Have you two put the world right?

NOREEN   *(Fumbling in sportsbag. Takes out knitting pattern. Checks a stitch. Checks pattern. Hums)* We're starting a revolution today.

LIONEL   Count me out. I want to win my match.

PRUDENCE   It's so peaceful. Do you think Angela and Dudley are ill or dead?

NOREEN   It means they're winning.

(Piercing scream. Enter Angela through auditorium, running with arms clasped to her bosom)

ANGELA   There's something down there. *(On stage. Looking down her front)* Come here you little bugger.

LIONEL Yes dear. *(Gets up. Trips over sportsbag and catapults into Angela's cleavage. Enter Violet running through auditorium)*

VIOLET I think she's got a bee down her wotsits. When I saw her cavorting round the base line, I thought you'd been teaching her a new serve, Noreen, but it must have been the bee.

LIONEL You'd better fetch Cattermole. *(Pronounced Ca-er-maul)*

VIOLET *(Tosses her head in contempt)* None of us is speaking to the referee.

NOREEN I'll go and don't drop any stitches. *(Hands knitting to Lionel)* and *(Jabbing her finger in Angela's direction)* and keep away from her erogenous zone. *(Exit Noreen through audience)*

ANGELA *(Looking down front of tennis dress)* The little bugger wouldn't leave me alone. It'll need an onion to get the swelling down.

VIOLET Come on. You'd better come to the changing room. If it's a bee it won't sting again, but if it's still down there, we'll have to set it free. *(Looks distastefully down Angela's cleavage)* Do put them away dear. Come along now. *(Exit Angela and Violet. Violet leads Angela by hand through audience. Angela follows like a lamb)*

LIONEL *(Holding knitting)* Lucky bee.

(Enter Dudley)

DUDLEY *(Towelling down. Drinks)* Ange got a bee in her bonnet?

LIONEL She has, but not in her bonnet.

DUDLEY Poor bee. She'll need an onion to get her swelling down. Li?

LIONEL *(Rummaging in sportsbag)* I've got elasticated bandages, senna pods *(Takes out a book)* a manual on safe Scottish dancing, *(Takes out a CD)* a CD of erotica violinists and some *(Takes out some girlie magazines then puts them away hurriedly)* magazines on bird-spotting round Little Buttox, but I ain't got no onions.

DUDLEY   I didn't know you were into birds? I think there's a bird-spotting group at the scout hut. Noreen wanted Wednesdays as a second dried flower evening but the hall is always booked out to something called Nightingale. She was rather annoyed.

LIONEL   I might pop down next Wednesday. I believe there are a lot of nightingales round Little Buttox.

(Enter Violet and Angela through audience)

DUDLEY   *(To Angela)* Has the swelling gone down?

ANGELA   Guess what's been erected? Two tents.

VIOLET   Two tents. Did you hear that, Lionel?

LIONEL   Too tense. I'm not too tense. Though I should be with all these bees, boobs and allusions to Bognor Beach. *(Lionel still holding knitting)*

VIOLET   Knitting suits you.

LIONEL   Why have two tents been erected?

ANGELA   They're holding sex tests in one and drugs tests in the other.

LIONEL   It's hard to decide which one to go in first. Do you have to take a sex exam?

ANGELA   Brussels are investing in veterans' tennis in the hope it'll keep us off the streets, cut pensioner vandalism and halve the cost of medical care for the elderly.

VIOLET   It's a sort of help the aged scheme.

ANGELA   Speak for yourself, dear.

DUDLEY   I thought the government and Lambeth Palace had decided we were all grey areas?

ANGELA   Overridden by Brussels, darling. Single currency was only the start. You're either male or female. No other possibilities considered.

PRUDENCE   I thought it had always been like that?

ANGELA Do we live on the same planet? I mean look at Duddie.

(Everyone looks at Dudley)

DUDLEY Don't look at me. I'm strictly your grey area.

ANGELA Duddie's different. He knits.

DUDLEY *(Taking knitting from Lionel.)* I'll finish that row for Noreen.

(Enter Marlon)

MARLON I've got to mow the court now.

VIOLET What, in the middle of a match?

MARLON Memo from Brussels.

PRUDENCE *(To Marlon)* Do they stop playing when you mow or do you have to dodge the balls?

MARLON Don't know about that. Memo didn't say.

VIOLET Look we're in the middle of drugs and sex tests. Not now, Marlon.

MARLON *(Exit Marlon muttering)* I'm not using my brain up with thinking when all they pays me is peanuts.

(Enter Noreen)

NOREEN *(To Angela and Violet)* I've just come from the referee. He wants to scratch you two. He says he wants to see you out of your draws

(Majestically Violet and Angela stash large handbags over their arms, pick up tennis rackets)

ANGELA Come Violet, my beloved and trusted enemy. *(Turning on Noreen)* At least she stabs me in the bust and not the bum.

VIOLET Let us make haste to the referee and make mince meat of his reject tennis balls. *(Exit Violet and Angela R to entrance to referee's office)*

NOREEN   *(Beckons them round her and bends head conspiratorially towards Lionel, Dudley and Prudence. They all grab chairs and sit in a group with Noreen in their midst)*   I've got a really good doctors and nurses story. One of my friends on the Women's Voluntary Tea Brigade has just told me; in the strictest confidence of course, so don't tell anybody.

(They all nod vigorously)

NOREEN   Actually we go to the same women's group and she works as a nurse at the same clinic as Angela. With *her* past, Angela's in the right job. We never really knew what happened.

DUDLEY   Let sleeping dogs lie.

NOREEN   Except buried bones have a nasty habit of working their way to the surface.

LIONEL   Get on with it Noreen. Don't leave us dangling.

NOREEN   If you're going to be rude I'm not telling you.

DUDLEY   Noreen we've not heard the end of that alcohol on club premises evening. We may yet get closed down. Do we need to know this?

LIONEL   Don't be a tease, Noreen.

NOREEN   Shut up. Where was I?

PRUDENCE   Doctors and nurses.

NOREEN   Oh yes. Wednesday was dirty linen day, so the nurses at the clinic counted out the number of uniforms to go to the laundry. When the van came just before knocking off time, there was one uniform missing. None of the nurses had taken it and there was only one customer all afternoon. Do you remember, Lionel, when we were young, people used to arrive at the tennis club with their balls in a string bag? Anyhow he went out with a wrapped object in one of those old-fashioned string ball bags. Well, as my friend said, you can't just out of blue ask a customer if you can please look in their string ball bag. Interesting isn't it?

UNISON   *(Bored)* Fascinating.

NOREEN   Don't you want to know who the customer was?

DUDLEY   Who was it?

NOREEN   Our referee, Cattermole.

UNISON   Ke-ter-me-lay!

NOREEN   I've not finished yet. You know my dried flower evenings in the scout hut?

LIONEL   I prefer you going to them rather than your women's group where you get stuffed full of radical ideas and I don't get my meal cooked.

NOREEN   My friend happened to see Cattermole lurking near the scout hut one Wednesday evening. She said she'd never seen anybody look so lurky. Anyway we've been trying to book another dried flower evening for Wednesdays, but it's always been booked out in the diary in the name of Nightingale. We thought it must be some local bird-spotting club.

LIONEL   Is it a private function, or can anyone join the group?

NOREEN   I would say it is a private function. Amazing how many nightingales there are round Little Buttox. I wish you *would* join, then it would get you from under my feet on my women's group evening, and I wouldn't have to rush back to throw your meal on the table. Anyway she followed Cattermole to his destination.

LIONEL   Did she have dirty raincoat on?

NOREEN   *(Ignores)* Cattermole went in the scout hut and my friend tiptoed round the back and stood on a crate.

LIONEL   Kinky.

NOREEN   Anyway she could just see through this high, cobwebby window. There were a load of men sitting in a circle on wooden chairs. She recognised the local blacksmith because of that big black beard, you know, that makes you want to pull it to see if it's real. She couldn't see much because one of them was smoking a pipe, oh and Dudley, another was knitting.

DUDLEY   Aah a man after my own heart.

NOREEN   And they all had nurses' uniforms on.

DUDLEY   Don't you just love a man in uniform.

LIONEL	Do you think Angela ought to know about this nurses' - sorry - bird-spotting circle?

NOREEN	Judging by her comment when we were talking about the men's team dressing in women's clothing, I think she already does. Angela seems to have extra-sensory perception when it comes to anything going on around the Buttox area.

LIONEL	*(Getting up)* Come on. I want to be casually looking at the gentlemen's draws when Ange and Vi sort out his discount tennis balls. I reckon he's in deep doo dah.

PRUDENCE	Oh do we have to? It's so comfortable here.

LIONEL	It's up to you, but you ain't seen nothing yet. Never mind doctors and nurses, if they chuck Ange and Vi out of their draws, you'll look back on this day as part of your education.

NOREEN	If you think hell hath no fury like a veteran tennis player beaten, wait till you see one chucked out of her draw. Hey you lot, wait for me. I must take the camcorder to record this for posterity.

LIONEL	Prosperity you mean. You never know we might be able to sell the video back to Cattermole. Could be worth a few bob.

(Lionel, Noreen, Prudence and Dudley group themselves around the referee's office R in the corner. They are obviously earwigging. Light comes on to show silhouette of Cattermole, the referee, seated. Violet on his right with racket raised over his head and Angela on his left. Outline of her bust clearly seen and near Cattermole's face. She is shaking her finger at him)

ANGELA	Look here, you slimy little toad. It's being put around that you're going to scratch me?

CATTERMOLE	Ladies it's like...

ANGELA	*(Banging table, voice rising)* I'm going to get this off my chest. I've got forty-eight hours to put my complaint through the proper channels, and I'll have you know I've liaised in some high places...

LIONEL	...and some pretty low places and Bognor Pier *(Snort)*

ANGELA	Now, allow me to recap. We've had flatulent oxygen tanks, groundsmen who can't handle things, bothersome bees and swollen boobs.

CATTERMOLE   I can see your point.

ANGELA   That's beside the point; do I stay in the tournament or not?

CATTERMOLE   Well it's like this.

VIOLET   *(Leaning close to him)* You wouldn't *dare* scratch us.

CATTERMOLE   *(Sounding strangled.)* Uhh...uhh... *(Squeezing a tennis ball.)*

VIOLET   It's no good sitting there squeezing tennis balls; they won't get any better; you're selling discount balls at best quality prices. They don't bloody bounce. Save 'em for your young ladies' coffee morning orgies.

ANGELA   *(Head close to Cattermole's. Menacing voice)* Now there are two ways we can handle this situation. I can simply pick up this microphone here *(Picks up microphone)* and inform the competitors of every one of your foibles, including a good doctors and nurses story, and *then* I shall simply make it up as I go along, and you know what a powerful imagination I have? Oh and I might mention that if anyone wants to join a local bird club on Wednesdays in the scout hut, they should sign the form at the referee's office *and* there's no charge for this marketing idea as to how to increase members at your little soirees.

CATTERMOLE   You wouldn't? They wouldn't believe you. They know *you*.

ANGELA   They know I work in *that* clinic and am in possession of sensitive information *(Slow and menacing)* like disappearing nurses' uniforms. Oh and if you get any more ideas about trying to get Little Buttox Club closed down so you can buy the land up cheap, I'm quite willing to sing as sweetly as a nightingale to the whole world including Mrs Cattermole, Little Boottox and Great Wollop Executive Committees, the EU in Brussels, the Lawn Tennis Association *and*... in a nurse's uniform if I have to.

VIOLET   It all sounds most dubious. No smoke without fire, I say. How *dare* you trifle with my affections, use me as a mole and then give me *re*ject tennis balls for my match, *Mr* Bunnykins.

ANGELA   On the other hand you could give us a tube of balls and Violet and myself will carry on as if nothing has happened. *(Starts juggling with his tennis balls)* You don't give the men rubbishy reject balls like you give us. Wouldn't it be awkward if your match and reject balls got mixed up? *(Starts flinging tennis balls around. Violet joins in. Tennis balls not reaching their high standards are chucked out of the referee's door. Enter Marlon, dodging tennis balls)*

MARLON   Would you like me to hose the courts down, Mr Cattermole?

CATTERMOLE   What in the middle of a tournament? Not now, Marlon.

MARLON   Good. Mother's expecting me to put a shelf up. *(Exit Marlon muttering)*

VIOLET   *(Angela and Violet continue flinging tennis balls around)* I fully intend to report the condition of your balls to Brussels.

LIONEL   By 'eck what a woman. Helen of Troy, Boadicea, Joan of Arc, Medusa, Cleopatra, Mrs Thatcher all rolled into one, and that chest...Ooh...*(Shuddering)*...What a spanking woman.

PRUDENCE   *(Reverently)* And Division Five ladies' captain.

LIONEL   As we stride bravely towards the twenty-first century, she should be preserved as an icon from this century. Is this - we ask ourselves - the way womanhood is heading? Future generations will build statues in her honour and her name will ring out across the courts of every tennis club in the land. *(Shuddering with ecstasy)* I'm beginning to understand what Violet's Cyril means by warrior women. What turns you on is the anticipation that at any moment she could sink her teeth into a soft and fleshy part and dominate you.

CATTERMOLE   *(Hands over a tube of tennis balls)*

VIOLET   *(Exits referee's office then changes her mind and pokes her head round his door)* And next time it won't just be your reject tennis balls bounding around your office. Come along Angela. *(To the strains of "The Arrival of the Queen of Sheba" marches majestically across back of stage and through auditorium. Angela trots obediently after her like a lamb. Little Buttox members by gentlemen's draws boards clap as the two warrior women go by)*

LIONEL *(To strains of Rimsky-Korsakov's "The Flight of the Bumble Bee" Lionel enters referee's office)* No need to get up, Ca-er-maul.

CATTERMOLE I wasn't going to. And it's Cat-ter-me-lay.

LIONEL *(Waves hand)* Whatever. Now when I was taking wine with the mayor...

CATTERMOLE *(Impatiently)* Look is this important? I've got a lot of matches to get on and a lot of balls to sort.

LIONEL If you don't spare me a moment, you might wish you had.

CATTERMOLE *(Tapping pencil on desk)* Oh get on with it then.

LIONEL When I was taking wine with the mayor we happened to be discussing the Little Buttox Council borrowing three courts at the Little Buttox Tennis Club on a Sunday evening, only we can't run to three courts because of restricting our restricted ladies. As a leading light of the Great Wollop Tennis Club, can you give us the green light to borrow one of your courts?

CATTERMOLE No.

LIONEL Is that a no 'no' or is it a 'can be bribed' no?

CATTERMOLE It's a no 'no.'

LIONEL I'm desperately searching for a local bird-spotting group. Can you help?

CATTERMOLE One court you said?

LIONEL Well blow me down and they say men aren't sensitive. I have a theory. Shall I tell you my theory?

CATTERMOLE No.

LIONEL I have a theory that life is all about people wanting something and people having something to hide and if you can get these two together, the sky's the limit. Now about that court...

CATTERMOLE Right I'll sleep on it.

LIONEL   Good to have these bonds between Great Wollop and Little Buttox. We tennis players are different and must back each other up against the world. By the way have you heard the nightingale this year?

NOREEN   *(Noreen approaches referee's office door)* Are we on yet?

LIONEL   Straight away my little plumpling. *(To Cattermole)* We'll tie up all our loose ends later.

(Lionel and Noreen exit to outside referee's doorway)

NOREEN   That was quick. We're usually down to play at ten and get on at four.

LIONEL   I think you'll find that'll never happen again. It's all about contacts and knowledge.

NOREEN   *(Folds arms and looks at him with a surprised but not displeased look)* You can be surprising sometimes. Surprising after all these years.

LIONEL   *(Puts tennis cap on back to front. Struts)* A fella needs to keep his mystery.

NOREEN   It all sounds very high-powered. Who are we playing?

LIONEL   *(Bends to look at draws outside referee's office)* Oh no.

NOREEN   *(Looking over Lionel's shoulder at draws)* Oh no.

(Prudence relaxing on grass. Lionel sits on chair and strums racket. Noreen picks up a tennis book. Enter a breathless Angela accompanied by Dudley)

ANGELA   Guess what, me and Dud are straight on. I've only just come off. Do you think I should go and complain to the referee?

(Little Buttox members cry as one) No.

ANGELA   He's got no balls, that Cattermole. At least I've got mental balls.

LIONEL   It takes balls to put four members of the Little Buttox Club on the same tennis court.

ANGELA   Guess who we're playing.

LIONEL   *(Grinning)* Us.

ANGELA   *(To Prudence)* Watch and learn, sweetheart.

PRUDENCE   Yes, Angela.

DUDLEY   *(Jumping up and down. Flexing knees)* Right. Match of the century. Get yourself psyched up.

LIONEL   *(Laying down row of caps. Looks at sun. Angles hand over eyes. Decides which to wear)*

NOREEN   *(Meditating in chair)*

DUDLEY   *(Puffs chest out. Stretching exercises. Running on spot)*

LIONEL   Wasting your time, Dudley, your knees will never go three sets. *(To Noreen)* I'll put this racket at one end and this one with the looser strings at t'other. What do you think, dear? I serve better with this and groundstroke better with this.

NOREEN   *(Hissing)* Not now Lionel. I'm tuning into my inner psyche.

LIONEL   *(Panicking)* We're haven't discussed tactics, darling.

NOREEN   *(Hissing)* Unless you get your balls over the net a bit more often, there aren't likely to be any tactics.

ANGELA   Call. *(Tosses a racket)*

LIONEL   Hang on a minute. *(Checks racket)*

ANGELA   Don't you trust me?

LIONEL   Never again after Bognor. You parked your car so the windscreen would dazzle a lefthander between two and three in the afternoon.

ANGELA   Don't expect me to control nature.

LIONEL   *(Looks at Angela appreciatively)* There are some laws of nature none of us can control.

NOREEN   *(Contemplative)* What is this thing you Buttox lot have got about Bognor. Lionel you seem to have been going to the Bognor tournament since, well since long before I knew you. I never get invited. Lionel you said you were at a conference?

ANGELA   Remember the first rule of doubles: Be in harmony with your partner.

NOREEN   Lionel?

LIONEL   *(Looking skyward)* I suppose, Dud, being a middle man you'll be practising your usual *divine interruptus* tactics?

(Dudley grins)

ANGELA   *(Tossing racket)* Call. P up or P down?

LIONEL   P up.

ANGELA   *(Looks at end of racket handle)* P down. We win. We'll serve first.

DUDLEY   *(Offended)* Well thanks for consulting me, Angela.

(Lionel and Noreen are arguing furiously)

DUDLEY   Amateurs, hoping to put us off by discussing tactics.

ANGELA   I don't think they're discussing tactics. I can hear things like '*Bognor Beach*;' '*ball bearing conferences*' and '*how the hell do I know where you are when I can only reach you on your mobile?*' Disharmony on the home front should work in our favour, all part of my master plan.

DUDLEY   I'm glad I'm on your team.

ANGELA   When you've had my upbringing, you *know* about guerrilla warfare. *(Shouts)* Are we starting, or what?

LIONEL   No need to be rude. We'll be with you in a moment. We're in a strategy meeting.

ANGELA   *(Handing balls to Dudley)* You serve first, Dud. You've got a strong nerve. When it comes to getting it in, you're one of God's chosen few.

DUDLEY   I think you should serve first. I don't know if I can get it in today. My mind goes all of a dither before a big performance. *(Wailing)* Ange why do I put myself through all this when I could be prodding away with my dibber in the parsnip plot.

ANGELA   You've got a perfectly nice house. I don't understand why you spend so much time in your parsnip plot?

DUDLEY   People are always calling at the house. They don't think to look in the parsnip plot.

ANGELA   *(Puts her arm round him and leads him to the front of the stage)* Be brave. It's the adrenaline flooding through your system. You need an outlet for aggression.

DUDLEY   I'm ready.

ANGELA   *(Hissing warningly)* The seeding of the Little Buttox Tournament and the whole year's pecking order rests on this. You won't get picked for the Great Wollop match if you don't perform today.

DUDLEY   You're such a great captain, I always *(Jumping up and down and clutching tennis racket)* respond *(Raises racket up)* when you get the whip out.

LIONEL   You two amateurs ready for a good thrashing?

NOREEN   *(Hissing to Lionel)* Don't make 'em angry. They always play better when they're angry.

(Exit Angela, Dudley, Lionel and Noreen. Prudence dozes peacefully. Gentle music. Enter Angela from wings. Dudley jumping up and down, follows)

ANGELA   One set down already. Honestly, Dud, you're buzzing around the net like an oversexed bumble bee.

DUDLEY   I feel like a rampant volleyer.

ANGELA   So do I, but where're we going to find one?

DUDLEY   I wish you'd stop hitting me in the back of the neck with your serve.

ANGELA   Why don't you bend right down. You look as though you're perched on a knitting needle.

DUDLEY I like to look tough. It frightens our opponents.

ANGELA *(Irritably)* Just jump up and down; I'll do the rest.

(As Angela and Dudley exit they bump into Lionel and Noreen coming from audience up onto the stage. Black looks all round)

NOREEN *(Enters with Lionel onto stage)* If you poach my balls one more time, I'm leaving home.

LIONEL It's the man's job to take as many balls as he can.

NOREEN If he can't get them in, then leave them to the woman. I don't mind, Lionel, if you're winning the point, but you're making a right old cock-up.

LIONEL I don't like you being profane. It's not ladylike.

NOREEN And another thing. I'm a woman, not a lady.

LIONEL Putting yourself in Angela's category?

NOREEN At least Angela's got balls. *(Exit Lionel and Noreen R)*

(Prudence alone on stage, relaxing in a deck-chair. Gentle music. Prudence is almost asleep. Enter Angela through auditorium. Pauses with thoughtful expression on her face at top of steps to stage. Prudence notices her)

PRUDENCE I thought you were playing?

ANGELA Lionel and Noreen are complaining to the referee about my line calling.

PRUDENCE That's surprising.

ANGELA Thank you. Dudley's taking an injury break so I don't know when we'll be back on. Mummy joining us?

PRUDENCE You know she hates tennis. I get a few token visits a year to my tennis activities. I sometimes think we get more out our friends...*(Looks at Angela)* well members of clubs... than our own families.

ANGELA Shame she doesn't share your interests.

PRUDENCE We don't have *anything* in common.

ANGELA   She does keep you down a lot. Don't you think she's a trifle possessive?

PRUDENCE   She loves me.

ANGELA   If you hold a little bird too tightly you might suffocate it.

PRUDENCE   Where is all this leading? I don't like giving you information. I know from Noreen how you use it.

ANGELA   I thought a woman of my experience might be able to help. I *have* been around you know.

PRUDENCE   So we all know.

ANGELA   *(Helping herself to a drink from the umpire stand)* Come on I'm not as bad as they make out.

PRUDENCE   I've never known you fail to winkle out anything you wanted to know. *(Defiantly)* Anyway she's not my real mum. I was adopted.

ANGELA   *(Drink goes down wrong way. Bent double in coughing fit. Spluttering. Puts drink down. Prudence gets up to thump her on the back)*

PRUDENCE   *(Concerned)* All right now?

ANGELA   Thanks. How old were you when you were adopted? *(Picks up Noreen's discarded knitting as Prudence sits down)*

PRUDENCE   I was a baby.

ANGELA   *(Knits a few stitches)* I've never known how old you are.

PRUDENCE   Thirty. Born on April Fool's Day. I can hear you thinking 'That figures.'

ANGELA   *(Silent as she concentrates on her knitting)*

PRUDENCE   Why have you gone quiet?

ANGELA   I was wondering what happened to your mother? Is she alive?

PRUDENCE   I don't know. I often dream about her. We're at a bus-stop. The bus draws up. She gets on. The doors close. She waves out of the window. *(Prudence waves then slowly covers her mouth with her hand)*...I never see her again...*(Pause)*...I didn't know you knitted, Angela?

ANGELA   I don't. *(Puts down knitting as if it is hot)* I'm screwing it up, like I do most things. *(Stands up, arms wrapped around herself as if cold. Back to audience)* Aren't you curious about your real mother?

PRUDENCE   Yes, but I don't want to meet her.

ANGELA   Supposing she wants to meet you?

PRUDENCE   She didn't want me then, why would she want me now? You're being very nice today; is something wrong?

ANGELA   *(Ironic laugh)* Keeping up the role of club bitch takes it out of you. Less stress being nice.

PRUDENCE   But why do you do it?

ANGELA   After tennis it's my next major sport. I like upsetting the hypocrites. At least I don't pretend to be respectable even if I'm probably more so than most of them.

PRUDENCE   But why do you like doing that?

ANGELA   Early problems.

PRUDENCE   When I said I was adopted...you seemed...well were you adopted?

ANGELA   Unfortunately my mother was my natural one. Perhaps you were the lucky one.

PRUDENCE   I don't think so. We're not close.

ANGELA   I would want to know about my real mother.

PRUDENCE   I do, but I shut it out. My real mother dumped me.

ANGELA   Mothers don't usually abandon their babies unless they've no alternative. There are young mothers who are still at school with no job and income and maybe can't count on their own mothers for help.

PRUDENCE   I suppose it must be terrible.

ANGELA   It is.

PRUDENCE   Oh?

ANGELA   It happened to me.

PRUDENCE   Oh?

ANGELA   I had to have Priscilla adopted.

PRUDENCE   *(Goes very still)* Excuse me, I must go, I don't feel very well. *(Hand over mouth, Prudence exits quickly)*

(Enter Dudley scurrying)

DUDLEY   Honestly, Ange, what have you said to upset Prudence now?

ANGELA   Nothing. Actually we were getting on rather well. Where's she gone?

DUDLEY   Marlon's looking after her in the groundsman's hut. Honestly, Ange, that tongue of yours.

ANGELA   Did you know she was adopted?

DUDLEY   Yes.

ANGELA   I was only trying to make her understand the other side by telling her about my past and Priscilla.

DUDLEY   *(Dudley shocked)* I didn't know your baby was called Priscilla.

ANGELA   And what's wrong with that?

DUDLEY   Prudence was always getting ragged at school.

ANGELA   What *is* it Duddie?

DUDLEY   Prudence's name was Priscilla but her classmates kept calling her Prissy so her name was changed to Prudence.

ANGELA   *(Howl of pain)* No.

DUDLEY   *(Stunned into silence)*

(End of Scene 1. Lights down)

SCENE 2

(Dudley and Prudence seated talking. It is as if we have come in part way through a conversation)

DUDLEY   ...but with so little genuine love in the world, can you afford to turn your back on the deepest relationship any of us ever know?

PRUDENCE   I don't believe it. I've spent years hating her. She's done nothing but belittle me. At least my moth...my present mother...isn't bitchy to me.

DUDLEY   There's a lot of good in Angela.

PRUDENCE   *(Gasp of disbelief)*

DUDLEY   I'm probably the only person who's seen the real Angela. She's honest and loyal and she's suffered; some people's defence is to attack the world before it attacks them.

(Enter Angela R hesitatingly. All former bravado gone. Waits at side of stage as if seeking permission to enter)

PRUDENCE   *(Looking at Angela)* I don't want to be on the same planet as *her*. *(Exit L quickly. Hurt etched on Angela's face. Dudley looks on helplessly)*

(Lights dip to indicate end of Scene 2)

SCENE 3

(Angela still in tennis clothes sits alone L of umpire stand. Head bowed in hands. Enter Prudence R Stops suddenly when she sees Angela. Look of hatred and partially turns to go. Angela takes tissue from handbag. Dabs eyes and nose. Sniffs as if she has been crying. Prudence watches. Her face softens. Angela looks up. Eye contact between two women)

ANGELA   Don't go. I've thought about you every night before going to sleep, wondering where you were and what you were doing.

PRUDENCE   You've ruined my life.

ANGELA   I thought it was for the best and you'd have a better life than I could give you.

PRUDENCE   I don't know who I am. I can't hold down a relationship. I feel so unwanted.

ANGELA   Oh believe me you were wanted. I couldn't tell my mother I was pregnant because...well.. I was desperate to keep you. How could I? She was an alcoholic. She just thought I was getting fat and cut my food down, so I went to auntie's in Bognor to have you and never went back.

PRUDENCE   Couldn't your auntie have helped?

ANGELA   She was elderly and crippled with arthritis and I had to look for a job. I couldn't support you so I had to have you adopted. You had a nice home didn't you.

PRUDENCE   *(Doubtfully)* Yes.

ANGELA   Well then?

PRUDENCE   It's awful when you don't feel you belong anywhere.

ANGELA   Well now you know where you come from. *(Looks appraisingly at Prudence)* You've got an attractive nose. Better than mine.

PRUDENCE   Am I like my father?

ANGELA   Yes, he was good looking.

PRUDENCE   You used to play at Bognor a lot when you were young, did you meet him there?

ANGELA   *(Sighs)* Ah Bognor, happy days. It's never the same when there's some part of you out there in the world somewhere and you don't know where. Every Christmas you think about them. Every anniversary of the birth is disturbing. Never any peace from it.

PRUDENCE   My father wasn't someone I know then? Not...Lionel?

ANGELA   Certainly not. We grew up together as teenagers. Played all the junior tournaments. When you've been good mates with someone; it's difficult to take them seriously.

PRUDENCE   It's not Dudley is it? I wouldn't mind if it was.

ANGELA   Good lord no. Dudley was always immersed in his knitting clubs and competitions.

PRUDENCE   Surely not Mr Cattermole; I don't like him.

ANGELA   Wouldn't touch him with a ten foot pole.

PRUDENCE   The only other one I can think of is Cyr...

ANGELA   Even I wouldn't risk Violet's wrath. Cyril was playing a small, bald Anthony to her Cleopatra even then. Your father was a good-looking boy. I don't know where he is now. *(Thinking)* We make mistakes when we're young and spend the rest of our lives thinking about them.

PRUDENCE   Did you ...?

ANGELA   ... love him? Yes, it wasn't a one-night stand. He never knew about you. What good would it have done? He'd just won a tennis scholarship to an American university. He hadn't any money.

PRUDENCE   It must have been hard for you 'cos you didn't have any warmth and cuddles either when you were young did you?

ANGELA   No.

PRUDENCE   I'm sure my mother loves me, but she can't show it. When you're a child and you're not cuddled you begin to think there's something wrong with you.

ANGELA   I want to be a mother to you, but I don't know how to start.

PRUDENCE   I've been so lonely. I've always looked to the club for my friends.

ANGELA   Trouble is we're a bit old for you aren't we?

PRUDENCE   No, that doesn't matter but why were you so horrible to me all the time? I admired you.

ANGELA   I don't know. Perhaps you being the same age group my own daughter would have been, brought home to me what I'd lost.

PRUDENCE   *(Sits down on chair R of umpire stand. Huge sigh. Puts hand up to face)* What do I say to my mother - I mean - my adopted mother. *(Begins to quiver as if some tension is draining from her. Angela watches. Gets up. Walks behind umpire chair to stand behind Prudence. Slowly extends hand to touch Prudence's shoulder. Prudence weeps quietly. Pulls away)*

ANGELA   *(Crouches beside chair. Puts her arms round Prudence's shoulders)* Don't let's lose any more time. Please. *(Prudence does not pull away from her)*

(Lights dim. Faintly Wagner's 'Ride of the Valkyries' begins to play)

VIOLET   *(Bustles up the side aisle of the auditorium and up the steps to front R Stops suddenly. Watches Angela and Prudence who do not notice her. Quietly)* Pretend I'm not here. *(Retreats down steps. Meets Dudley scurrying from rear of auditorium)*

VIOLET   Dudley, dear boy, I do believe we've got an outbreak of...vegetarianism in the club.

DUDLEY   There's nothing wrong with that.

VIOLET   You know what I mean.

DUDLEY   I don't. I've got a lot on my mind at the moment what with the knitting competition pending.

VIOLET   You know...women...women in sensible shoes.

DUDLEY   What about them?

VIOLET   Oh Dudley where have you been all your life?

DUDLEY   Oh...you mean bosom pals?

VIOLET   Prudence and Angela. Well it doesn't surprise me that Angela licks both sides of the stamp but with Prudence ... well I thought they hated each other.

DUDLEY   Prudence and Angela. Hardly. You know all about Angela's past.

VIOLET   Not the bit about girls, although we had quite a lot of it at St Buttox.

DUDLEY   The baby Angela had adopted turns out to be Prudence.

VIOLET   Good lord ... who's the sire? Not you surely?

DUDLEY   Don't be silly Violet, I wouldn't have had the time what with knitting, tennis and my career.

VIOLET   Seriously, don't you know who the father is? I'd have thought in your position you'd have access to sensitive information.

DUDLEY   It must have been someone who used to go to the Bognor tournament.

VIOLET   Well it couldn't be Cyril. He assures me he's never been to Bognor. Anyway I don't know where Angela found the time for rumpy-pumpy. She and I always went all the way to the final; I thrashed her then... just like I did today.

DUDLEY   Look for the moment keep it under your hat about this mother/daughter thing until they decide to go public.

VIOLET   Of course, dear boy. All in the strictest confidence. Must dash. Got to pick up some sugar before Mrs Floggitt shuts up shop. *(Exit Violet to rear of auditorium. Exit Dudley to wings R)*

(End of Scene 3. Lights down)

SCENE 4

(Enter Dudley R with Angela. Enter Prudence L)

ANGELA *(Sitting down L of umpire stand whilst Dudley messes about in his sports holdall at foot of umpire stand)* Prudence will you partner me in the match tomorrow?

PRUDENCE *(Sits down R of umpire stand. Starts laughing in slightly hysterical manner, then uncontrollably as if tension flooding out of her.* Are you serious? I thought the team had already been chosen?

ANGELA Oh I think Violet's eloped or something with Cattermole.

PRUDENCE Surely not.

ANGELA Well, anyway she told Mrs Floggitt, in the strictest confidence of course, that she's going with him to *Spitzenfahrt* - with the club's best interests at heart naturally - to discuss their twinning with Little Buttox and Great Wollop.

(Enter Marlon L carrying scarifying rake)

MARLON I've come to scarify the courts. Memo from Brussels. *(Dudley, Angela, Prudence start laughing)* What did I say?

DUDLEY Nothing, Marlon, you've just come in the middle of a catharsis.

MARLON Memo didn't say nothing about no catharsis. Anyway my doctor says I shouldn't scarify in my condition.

ANGELA I shouldn't think your mother would approve of you scarifying either.

DUDLEY Don't you think you ought to go and put that shelf up for your mother?

MARLON *(Sits down. Fiddles with wires of scarifying rake)* No, I'll do it when I've attended to more important matters.
Are you all right, Prudence? You still look so pale?

PRUDENCE *(Overbrightly)* I'm fine, Marlon, really. We're just discussing private things. I'll tell you all about it later.

MARLON   Mother says I shouldn't tamper with women's private things.

DUDLEY   *(Packing tennis things into sports holdall. 'Sussex by the Sea' gently playing)* What a lovely evening; it's all so English. When it's nine o'clock in the evening and I'm away from home I often think, it's *Horlicks* time at Little Buttox and wonder what the members are doing. There's a continuity of life in the clubs and a knowledge that's passed from one generation of players to the next.

ANGELA   And the feuds go on.

MARLON   Mrs Floggitt said you two thrashed Lionel and Noreen; is that right?

DUDLEY   We did, Marlon, we certainly did. I really don't know how we can go home now after all that's happened today. Shall we all go to the Pat and Punch Party tonight?

MARLON   I don't think Prudence will go if I go.

PRUDENCE   *(Touches him on the shoulder)* Oh Marlon that's not true, but promise not to mention your mother; I can't cope with any more mothers today. *(Looks at Angela who looks back and smiles)*

DUDLEY   Angela would you do me the honour of accompanying me to the Pat and Punch Party?

ANGELA   *(Quietly)* I'd like to, Dudley, but *(Looking at Prudence)* I think I ought to go home now.

DUDLEY   *(Disappointed)* Oh well I'd better get changed. *(Exits to changing rooms)*

PRUDENCE   *(Fiercely to Angela)* Oh no you don't. You'll sweat it out with me at the Pat and Punch Party. And why don't you make Dudley's day and say 'yes'.

ANGELA   *(Shouting)* Dudley. I'd love to go out with you tonight.

DUDLEY   Wonderful. Shall I pick you up after work? *(Enter Dudley dressed as a vicar. Takes Angela's hand. Moves to front of stage. Marlon holding scarifying rake stands awkwardly behind Prudence. Prudence takes his hand. They move to front of stage. Prudence and Angela are between the two men)*

PRUDENCE   *(To Angela)* You always did like men in uniform? Can I borrow your black leather outfit tonight?

ANGELA   *(Puts arm around Prudence's shoulder)* You can *have* it. It's a bit young for me.

(Four jump in a startled way as oxygen tank falls over and emits raspberry sound. They look behind them and laugh)

CURTAIN

YOU CAN'T BE SERIOUS

GROUND PLAN

Act 1

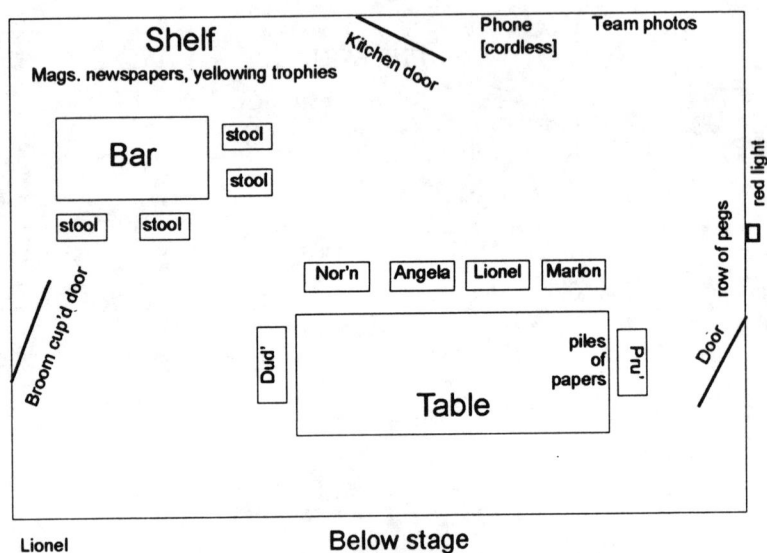

Shelf
Mags. newspapers, yellowing trophies

Kitchen door

Phone [cordless]   Team photos

Bar

stool
stool
stool
stool

red light

row of pegs

Door

Broom cup'd door

Nor'n | Angela | Lionel | Marlon

Dud'   Table   piles of papers   Pru'

Lionel on phone
Chair

Below stage
Green baize, short tennis net, soft balls, people playing short tennis prior to curtain up and during interval

YOU CAN'T BE SERIOUS

GROUND PLAN

Act 2

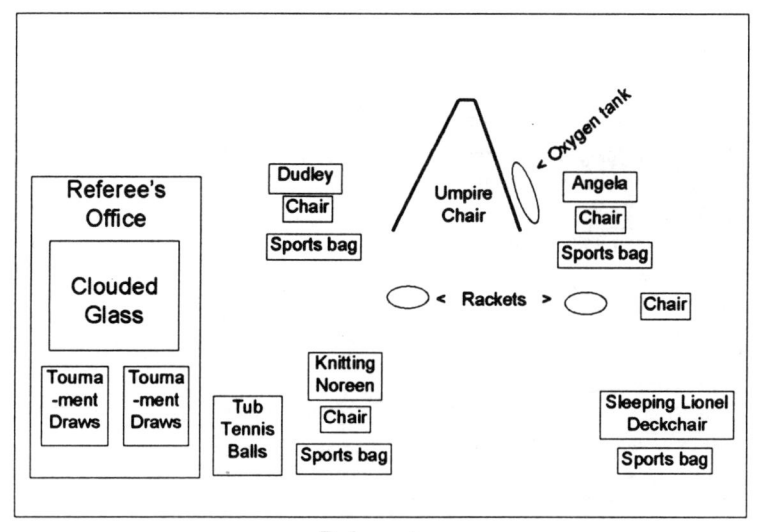

- Referee's Office
- Clouded Glass
- Tourna-ment Draws
- Tourna-ment Draws
- Dudley Chair
- Sports bag
- Umpire Chair
- Oxygen tank →
- Angela Chair
- Sports bag
- < Rackets >
- Chair
- Tub Tennis Balls
- Knitting Noreen Chair
- Sports bag
- Sleeping Lionel Deckchair
- Sports bag

Below stage
Green baize on which short tennis is being played in interval

II

FURNITURE AND PROPERTY LIST

PRIOR TO CURTAIN UP

Below Stage:
Green baize. *On it:* Short tennis set comprising net, four bats, several soft short tennis balls.

ACT I

On Stage:
Trestle table. *On it:* Piles of untidy files.
Chairs - hotchpotch of design - look like cast offs from members' homes.
Shelf. *On it:* magazines, newspapers, yellowing trophies.
Row of clothes hanging pegs.
Bar stools. Four.
Cordless telephone mounted on wall.
Team photos.
Loo brush.
Ashtrays.
Litter on floor.
Little Buttox Gazette - several copies.
Little Buttox Lawn Tennis Club agenda - several copies.
Bottles of alcoholic drink.
Drinking glasses, beer mugs.
Coffee and tea mugs.
Cake plates.
Paper serviettes.

Personal.
ANGELA: Red motorcycle helmet, leather jacket, leather skirt, decolletage top, slingbag high heel shoes, handbag, mirror, cosmetic bag, nail varnish, manicure set, lipstick.
DUDLEY: Bicycle, lock and chain, cycle clips, cloak, clerical gown, knitting.
PRUDENCE: Shorthand notebook, pencils, bag of files/papers, motorcycle helmet, hankerchief, smock, black leather trousers, white leather jacket, glittering decolletage top.
NOREEN: Cake tin, chocolate cake, briefcase, carrier bags, old-fashioned handbag.
LIONEL: Easel on which flip chart can rest, extending ruler, amusing drawings, watch.
VIOLET: Wooden handrail, large notices reading *Pate and Punch Party* and *Fondue Party*, suitcase, horse harness, riding whip, colander.
MARLON: Book, cap.

INTERVAL

Below stage.
   Green baize. *On it:* short tennis set comprising net, four bats, several soft balls.

ACT II

On stage:
   Umpire chair.
   Cans of soft drinks.
   Deckchairs - two.
   Canvas chairs - four.
   Sports holdalls.
   Tennis rackets.
   Tub of tennis balls.
   Tournament draws affixed to noticeboards.
   Oxygen cylinder affixed to umpire chair.
   Loudspeaker system.

Personal:
   ANGELA: Canister of deodorant, knickers with imprint of hand on each buttock, towel, hankerchief, handbag, tissues.
   NOREEN: Knitting and pattern, book.
   CATTERMOLE: Microphone, pencil.
   DUDLEY: Banana.
   MARLON: Screwdriver, length of toilet paper, scarifying rake.
   LIONEL: Book, CD, Girlie magazines.
   VIOLET: Handbag.
   PRUDENCE: Summer dress.

YOU CAN'T BE SERIOUS

MUSIC/SOUND PLOT

ACT I

SCENE I

To open.
   Sound - Tennis balls being struck.

At cue.
   Sound - Bicycle squeak.
   Music - *Dance of the Sugar-Plum Fairy* (Tchaikovsky)
   Sound - Motorbike.
   Music - *The Typewriter*. (Leroy Anderson)
   Sound - Car.
   Music - *One man went to mow* (Traditional Folk Song)
   Sound - Motorbike.
   Music - *Arrival of the Queen of Sheba* (Handel)
   Sound - Telephone.
   Music - *Flight of the Bumble Bee* (Rimsky-Korsakov)
   Music - *Love and Marriage* (Sammy Cahn/Jimmy van Heussen))
   Sound - Cake tin drops.
   Music - *Ride of the Valkyries* (Wagner).
   Sound - Splash.

INTERVAL

   Sound - Tennis balls being struck.

ACT II

At cue.
   Sound - Raspberry.
   Sound - Slap.
   Sound - Raspberry.
   Music - *Arrival of the Queen of Sheba* (Handel)
   Music - *Flight of the Bumble Bee* (Rimsky-Korsakov)
   Music - *Sussex by The Sea* (W. Ward-Higgs)

To end.
   Sound - Raspberry.

LIGHTING PLOT

ACT I
SCENE I

To open.
　　Clubhouse on stage dimly lit.
　　Outside club entrance L. - red light.
At cue.
　　Dudley hangs cloak - switches clubhouse lights on.
　　Telephone rings. Prudence gets up to answer.
　　Lionel's hallway below stage R. lit.
　　Lionel concludes conversation. Lights off below stage R.

ACT II
SCENE I

To open.
　　Bright sunshine.
At cue.
　　Referee's office R. lit. Figures seen in silhouette.
　　Referee's office R. - lights off.
　　Referee's office lit.
　　Exit Violet, Angela, Marlon, Lionel. Lights off.

SCENE 2

To open.
　　Later in day. Sun not so bright.
At cue.
　　End of Scene 2. Lights down.

SCENE 3

To open.
　　Lights on but not so bright as later in day.
At cue.
　　End of Scene 3. Lights down.

SCENE 4

To open.
　　Dusk.

Each one of the scripts published by The Playwrights Puhlishing Company has been carefully vetted before it reaches you and has been chosen because it is believed to contain something special.

If you wish to know more about our plays and would like one of our catalogues or are yourself a new author please write enclosing SAE to the address given in the front of this book.